NOTHING TO TELL

Extraordinary Stories *of* Montana Ranch Women

DONNA GRAY

with a foreword by

LINDA PEAVY *and* URSULA SMITH

TWODOT®

GUILFORD, CONNECTICUT
HELENA, MONTANA
AN IMPRINT OF GLOBE PEQUOT PRESS

A · **TWODOT**® · **BOOK**

All photos from the Library of Congress.
Map: Daniel Lloyd © Morris Book Publishing, LLC
Project editor: Meredith Dias
Text design: Elizabeth Kingsbury
Layout: Kirsten Livingston

Library of Congress Cataloging-in-Publication Data

Gray, Donna, 1927–
  Nothing to tell : extraordinary stories of Montana ranch women /
Donna Gray ; foreword by Linda Peavy and Ursula Smith.
    p. cm.
  ISBN 978-0-7627-7909-3
  1. Women ranchers—Montana—Interviews. 2. Women
pioneers—Montana—Interviews. 3. Women farmers—Montana—
Interviews. 4. Ranch life—Montana—History. 5. Frontier and
pioneer life—Montana. 6. Farm life—Montana—History. 7.
Montana—Social life and customs. 8. Montana—Biography. 9.
Oral history—Montana. 10. Interviews—Montana. I. Title.
  F730.G73 2012
  978.6—dc23

                              2011046235

Printed in the United States of America

10 9 8 7 6 5 4 3 2 1

For John

and for the women who shared their stories with me.

I wish I could put this book in your hands.

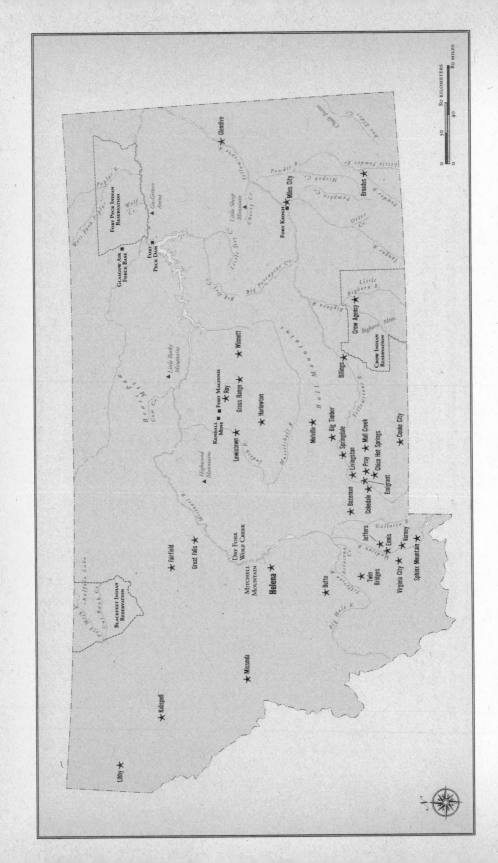

CONTENTS

Contents

FOREWORD

Thirty years ago, Donna Gray set up her tape recorder on the kitchen table of the first of the twelve Montana ranch women whose oral histories make up the chapters of this book. At the time she might or might not have been aware that she was among the relatively few academic and lay historians who had begun capturing the voices and recording the stories of rural women whose day-to-day experiences were part of a rapidly disappearing way of life.

Gray's first interview took place in 1982, almost a year before Susan Armitage challenged historians to examine the "extraordinariness of ordinary lives," to step back from their work on the lives of women known to be groundbreakers and to look for—and at—the experiences of women whose lives were a vital part of the unfolding story of the earlier West. As Armitage issued that challenge, Gray was facing a challenge of her own. Convinced as she was of the importance of recording the experiences of her cohort of Montana ranch women,

she found her prospective subjects reluctant to be interviewed, convinced as they were that the "ordinariness"
of their own everyday lives meant they had done nothing worth talking about, that they had nothing to tell.

As the stories in this book attest, nothing could
have been further from the truth. Even the most casual
reader will soon realize that these are important stories.
And those with an interest in western history, whether
living and working among us now or historians in the
future, will be grateful to Gray for taking the time to
record these words. Too often we don't stop to prompt
our mothers, grandmothers, and great-grandmothers to
share their experiences. We're too engaged in our own
lives, too busy, too impatient.

But Donna Gray took the time to sit with these
women, to prompt their musings with appropriate questions, and to listen with a sensitive ear as the memories began to flow. She did us one more favor. Besides
capturing these stories for our enjoyment and education,
she captured each woman's unique voice in verbatim
transcriptions of the interviews. As we read the words,
we can actually hear the voices. And these voices engage
us, not only for their distinctive patterns and idiomatic
phrasings, but also for the stories they convey—stories
that offer rich detail concerning early-twentieth-century
ranch life. In some cases, that detail attaches to work
within traditional gender roles—bearing and rearing
children, milking cows, churning butter, raising a garden, cooking on a woodstove, doing laundry in a washtub, teaching in a one-room schoolhouse. But, often as

not, the stories take us into the nontraditional work demanded of ranch wives: shocking grain, herding cows, and hunting game. Ethel Briggs tells us of building a barn's rock foundation with her own hands; we learn that, at age eighty, Bea Murray was still branding her own calves.

We hear stories that span a lifetime. Madge Walker recalls the joy of trips to town, where a child could help herself to gingersnaps out of a barrel in the general store. Urma Taylor tells of the delight that came from playing with her "little frogs," which took the place of the dolls she didn't have. Two of the women describe shivarees, the high-spirited, late-night processions of close friends and family members to the home of a newly married couple. Helen Wonder shares memories of her honeymoon at ten thousand feet on Sphinx Peak in the Madison Valley, where her groom was hunting bears for the government. Clara Nickelson tells of settling up grocery bills only once a year—in the fall after the family's cattle were sold.

Some of these stories give insight into historical events of the era: Marie Converse describes anti-German sentiment and its consequences in Lewistown, Montana, after World War I. She also tells of her family's participation in a federal resettlement program during the Great Depression, of the ranchers' ambivalence about relying on government assistance, and of local residents' prejudices against the "resettlers." Eva DePuy blames the abdication of Edward VIII of England for the failure of her fledgling mink business; she and her husband had counted on the coronation to spark a surge in the market, which bottomed when that coronation never took place.

While most of Gray's ranch women mention in passing their involvement in "men's work," Marie describes in great detail the tedious and complex steps involved in haying. Her description is a veritable how-to manual on the lost art of haying. "It didn't take me long to learn to build a good stack of hay" would have sufficed for most women who mentioned their participation in such tasks, yet Converse's delight and pride in her work comes through in her precise recall of each step.

Converse's enthusiasm for haying is matched—even exceeded—by Lillian Mehlhoff's infatuation with chickens. Giving short shrift to all other topics, Mehlhoff provides us with a litany of breeds, from "the heavy breeds, the meat breeds . . . Buff Orpingtons, Red Rhode Island, Wyandotte" to the laying breeds like the leghorn. The hatching, feeding, and care of chicks; the washing, sorting, and sale of eggs; the butchering, scalding, plucking, singeing, and dressing of chickens—to her, all of it is worthy of the telling.

Converse's exposition on the finer points of haying, Mehlhoff's lengthy treatise on every aspect of raising chickens: Do we care about these details? Maybe not, but we do care about the women who share them. We have come to know these women, to recognize their voices, to visualize their worlds, to sense their excitement at finally being able to tell *someone* about the everyday things that were so central to their lives.

In so many ways the narratives Donna Gray captured exemplify the extraordinariness of ordinary lives, leaving no doubt about the worth and the wisdom of the women who thought they had "nothing to tell."

—*Linda Peavy and Ursula Smith*

ACKNOWLEDGMENTS

This book would not have existed without the ongoing encouragement of my husband. Even during his last illness, when he no longer had a grasp of daily reality, he retained some idea of the work's importance to me. Once, in insisting that he could do the vacuuming in my stead, he said, "I can do this. You . . . you go make a book."

I also wish to thank Dawn Curry, my guardian angel, who began this project doing secretarial work for me but who became so much, much more. My thanks as well to Laurie Mercier, now of Washington State University, Vancouver, who was the oral historian at the Montana Historical Society when I first came to the state in the early '70s and who enlisted me as a freelance worker. If I am comfortable in the field of oral history, it is due to her guidance. My gratitude goes as well to Teresa Jordan, whose kindnesses sustained me in the early years of the work, and to Ursula Smith and Linda Peavy, who have supported me throughout the project. And, finally, my thanks to Erin Turner, who is, after all, the one who took this manuscript in with great enthusiasm and brought it to print.

Portions of Urma Taylor's and Madge Walker's interviews appear in Lillian Schlissel and Catherine Lavender's *Western Women's Reader* (2000); brief passages from Urma Taylor's and Ethel Briggs's stories are found in *Leaning into the Wind* (1997), a collection of women's writings edited by Linda Hasselstrom, Gaydell Collier, and Nancy Curtis; Ethel Briggs and Madge Walker appear in Linda Peavy and Ursula Smith's *Pioneer Women* (1996); and Kaia Cosgriff and Urma Taylor appear in Peavy and Smith's *Frontier Children* (1999).

INTRODUCTION

"It's a good old life, if you can stand it," says Eva DePuy, one of the dozen Montana ranch women whose oral histories are presented in this book. That one statement seems to me to capture the spirit of the women who shared their life stories with me.

I first became interested in oral histories after interviewing several working women in California for a writing project and later when working as a contract interviewer for the Montana Historical Society. The society was then doing an oral history series on occupations in Montana, and after hearing the histories of several men in the ranching, railroad, and timber industries, I began to wonder what their wives would have to say.

At the time, I lived on a ranch in Montana's Paradise Valley, and so I began by talking to several neighboring ranch women. Their stories were so compelling that I wove them into a reader's theater, *Four Ladies from*

Pray. Performed locally, the play was well received.* Soon people were coming up to me and saying, "I know this wonderful woman, you've got to talk to her." Before long, such suggestions were flying out of the trees; it seemed that everyone knew someone I should interview.

When I approached the women suggested to me as possible subjects for the proposed work, almost every one of them protested that she had "nothing to tell," that her life had been unremarkable. In each case, I simply asked the woman if she would submit to an interview and then let me be the judge.

In the end, their stories all proved worthy of telling. I conducted the first of the twelve interviews in 1982, the last one six years later. The women lived primarily in the western part of the state, most of them in Park and Madison Counties, though a few lived on the plains in central Montana. I interviewed each one over several visits, all but one of them in their own homes, often around the kitchen table.** No one else was ever present. If, for instance, a husband came in for the midday meal during the interview, we broke off until he had left again. Some of the women were initially more forthcoming than others, but eventually they all opened up. I usually found that once I got them talking, it was hard to get them to stop, and by the time the interviews were

---

* The four women whose stories became a part of the reader's theater are Ethel Briggs, Urma Taylor, Florence Lyall, and Madge Walker.
** Because she didn't want her husband "to know what she was up to," Urma Taylor opted to be interviewed at my home rather than her own.

finished, each woman seemed to feel a sense of pride in what she had to share.

I initially typed out each interview word for word, then made some revisions to keep the story flowing smoothly. I did my best to capture the spirit of each woman: the way she spoke, her phrases and accent. I sent each one a copy of her transcript and told her she could make any corrections she felt necessary. By the time I had a dozen solid histories, I reluctantly decided that it was time to end the process and seek a publisher.

Over the years, I had to set this project aside several times when life had other plans for me, but I am pleased to finally have all of the histories appear together in this book. It seems important to hear the stories of these women because the life they led is disappearing altogether. We now have little or no knowledge of the way laundry was done or what it is like to carry water a quarter of a mile, work without electricity, and somehow fit all those indoor and outdoor chores into a single day. Having known a different way of life, these women have a unique perspective to offer us.

I think one of the most important messages they have for us is that we should enjoy what we have. In delivering that message, they chastise us a bit. They were the epitome of thrift. They saved, reused, and made do with what they had. As a whole, they were put out with us and our "fancy equipment." Some observed that while people today have every modern convenience, they still complain about their "heavy workload." They felt that the modern child is spoiled with far too many material possessions. One described the country as "gettin' more like a Sodom and Gomorrah outfit," with everyone looking only for a good time.

Another common thread was their nostalgia for the feeling of community that people once knew. Community events like holiday gatherings and dances were eagerly awaited all year. And more time was given to visiting among neighbors. Even without an invitation, you could count on your neighbor to offer you a meal and a place to stay. People just "dropped in." As one of the women said, "You were likely as not to come home and find your house full of somebody." They regretted that a deep appreciation for friends and neighbors was being lost.

These women loved Montana, where often their mothers did not, having come from somewhere else, and often their children did not, growing up and moving on to somewhere else. These women found comfort in the rural life and often couldn't imagine living any other way. The interviews gave them a way to assess their lives, to come to marvel at themselves, at how hard they had worked and at what they had accomplished.

I hope you enjoy their stories. I think you will agree with me that these twelve women certainly had something to tell.

—Donna Gray

HELEN CLARK WONDER

"The mountains, they're part of me."

Helen Clark Wonder was born in Varney, Montana, on December 2, 1910. A small, plump woman with a good sense of humor, Helen had endured more hardships than most: family illnesses, poverty, and an early widowhood. She sat at her kitchen table in a cotton housedress and told of her hardscrabble life.

The day I was born, Mama walked down to Lizzie Vetters's house, a mile or so down the road, and she started into labor. My father was elk hunting near West Yellowstone. When Dad came along, Lizzie said, "George, you better go get some baby clothes, Lily's going to have the baby." He went on up to where they lived to get the baby clothes, and when he come back, I was born.

I was the second baby. I had a sister who was born in 1908. She died with pneumonia in 1910, and then I was born ten months later. As long as my mother lived, she grieved for my sister that she had lost.

I s'pose the first I can really remember, we moved across the Madison River to Trail Crick, where my Grandfather Carkeek lived. He had a small log house, two rooms and an enclosed porch. Grandpa slept on the porch, and we slept in the bedroom part. By that time I had a brother. I was almost two years older than him. The thing that stands out in my memory was that Christmas. I got a little set of blue dishes and a doll, but it didn't seem like Christmas 'cause we didn't have a Christmas tree.

At first Dad worked for ranchers. He had taken up a homestead, and he was building our house. I can't remember the move from my grandfather's to our house, but I remember it seemed like we had moved into a really big house because it was *four big rooms*.

We were down in a little bowl there, with the hills and the Indian Crick peaks all around us. We had a dining room window that faced out on the peaks, and I remember, as a child, lookin' out, especially in the wintertime, when the sun'd be goin' down, those mountains would be a pink like you'd think was good enough to eat. I've always looked to the mountains for my help and strength. The mountains, they're part of me.

My dad was from a big family; there was twelve children. Two of them stayed in Missouri; the other ten came to Montana to live.

My Clark grandparents lived south of us, and my Uncle Virge lived up on the hill, a mile above us. Over on another hill, north and east of there, Uncle Fred and Uncle Bruce homesteaded. There was Grandpa and three homesteads of his sons right around him.

We saw each other every week at least. It was a happy time for everybody to go to each person's place and be together.

My Aunt Blythe always cooked Thanksgiving dinner, my grandmother the Christmas dinner, and my mother the New Year's dinner. In those days, the children waited 'til the grown-ups had finished a meal before they could sit down and eat. I can remember that was hard, to wait 'til the grown-ups ate, because they took their time.

We had chicken or wild meat, because all of the Clark boys were great hunters. Chicken, elk, deer, and they got a few mountain sheep, too. Mountain sheep is the best wild meat there is. It tastes more like domestic meat, different from deer and elk. It's marbleized like beef. Probably not as good for you, but it's better tasting. I haven't had any mountain sheep for twenty-five or thirty years now, but I can't remember that it has a mutton flavor at all. It's very good.

Helen's Grandfather Clark, her father, and two of her uncles formed a ranching partnership. They, like so many Montana ranchers, suffered great losses during the terrible winter of 1918–19.

The first winter they had sheep, the winter of 1918 and '19, Dad hauled hay and corn from Norris on a drag sled, a sled with a big long bed on it. Let's see . . . we were twenty-five miles up-country, and it's sixteen miles to Norris from Jeffers. It took two or three days. And the hay was terrible! It was cut on sloughs in Minnesota and was full of ice. We lost eleven hundred sheep that winter.

They fed the sheep over at our place because we had a big field that Dad always planted in wheat and oats. They fed the sheep there, and I can remember my mother standin' at the window cryin' at all these dead sheep. It kept two men busy, just skinnin' sheep. They starved to death. [The sheep were unable to eat the icy hay.] They hauled corn, too, but it didn't get 'em through. That was a real setback to Grandpa, Dad, and his two brothers. All they got was a few dollars for the sheep pelts. Sad, sad to see all those dead sheep. A hard winter, a terrible hard winter.

During that same winter, Helen and her brother attended the Indian Creek School, which was more than a mile from their home.

Sometimes when we walked to school, it would be thirty degrees below zero. We had about a mile and a half to walk. If we could get ready in time, we could ride with the man a-goin' to the timber with a sled. That was a great thing, to get a ride to school on those cold mornings.

Mama would make me wear boys' overalls, and of course we all wore long underwear. And I had the old black sateen bloomers. I can still smell the dye in those bloomers! We'd wrap scarves around our faces, and we would run and we would walk and we would run until we got to school, but we'd be almost frozen.

After we got a half a mile from the house, we could walk in the lane the rest of the way, so we knew we was all right as long as we stayed between the two fences. But goin' that first half mile was pretty rough sometimes.

There was times when, if there was a little wind with the cold temperatures, they kept us at home. It was too cold; it was too dangerous.

One snow that I remember, I was in the third grade and we walked to Trail Crick School, which was prob'ly two miles. We had summer school, from April 'til the end of October. My brother and I were the only two that went from our direction that day. It wasn't bad in the morning, but we got lost comin' home.

This terrible storm had come up. We walked across fields, no lanes or anything to follow. When it kind of broke once, I could see we were half a mile toward the county road. We should have been up next to the hills. We finally got to Grandma's, and she bawled us out good.

"Where have you children been? It's late, it's goin' to be dark before you get home."

I don't know why she didn't have one of my uncles go with us, because it was still open country from there to our place. We started out. We got past Grandpa's fence, the boundary line between us and him. I could hear my mother calling. She kept calling; we kept answering. We got together and she got us home. She'd set the lamp in the window so she could see the light. And tied my little brother in the high chair so he couldn't do anything while she was gone. That lamp was a welcome sight when we got to where we could see it.

Helen and her brother didn't get sick after their ordeal, but Helen remembered the home remedies her family used, each one more difficult to take than the last.

When we got a chest cold, the remedy was turpentine and lard with a flannel on our chest. Honey and butter and vinegar—we didn't have lemons—sometimes whiskey in it, for a head cold. Ours was always home remedies. Sore throat: blowed sulphur in your throat. That gritty old stuff on your teeth! Grandma was a great believer in acifidity. That was the stinkinest stuff you ever smelled. She'd fix it up in little sacks with a string for us to wear around our necks so we wouldn't get the flu. Or, if we stopped by on the way to school, she'd crumble it up in a teaspoon of whiskey and give it to us to take. And it tasted just as bad as it smelled. We got to where we learned not to stop by Grandma's on the way to school.

Sometimes they'd give us for colds two or three drops of turpentine on a spoonful of sugar. Or two or three drops of coal oil on sugar. I guess they worked. We never had a doctor when we were kids. I was twelve or fourteen the first time we had a doctor. I was fifteen when I had my tonsils out, and I'd been to the doctor several times about my throat, because I was about to have mastoid. They decided if they took my tonsils out, maybe that'd help the mastoid, and it did.

There was a flu epidemic during World War I. I had an aunt that had it real bad. The doctor said, "Put saucers of carbolic acid around to kill the germs in the room." That sounds silly today, but that's what the doctor told them to do.

"Don't let anybody in." Grandma or Grandpa didn't get it, but it seems like maybe a cousin did. Dad went over to see my aunt, and Grandma said, "No, George, you can't go in. You've got Lil and those little children, and you'll get the flu." Dad said, "As long as I'm smokin' my pipe, I won't get the flu." He smoked his pipe while he's there, and he never got the flu.

So many people died with it. The poor old doctor we had here, I guess he finally got somebody to drive with him. He got a car, and he'd sleep between calls and have this fellow drive for him. He was a good doctor. One of his remedies was to give people good whiskey. It was that turned him into an alcoholic. He died over at Warm Springs [the state psychiatric hospital, established in 1895].

My mother used to have seizures, and we children would stand around and cry. Twice I sent for my grandmother. Mama had some pills up in the cupboard. She had a table under the cupboard, and when she got up there to get the pills, she went into the seizure. When she fell back, she hit the corner of the cupboard door and cut her head open. When I saw the blood, I was really scared. I sent my oldest brother to get my grandmother.

By the time she got there—Grandmother never hurried in her life—Mom was up, doin' the work. She'd come out of it, but she had a pretty good gash in the back of her head. Another time, she went into a seizure, and her head got caught between two rods on a brass bed. I couldn't get her out for a while, and that time I sent for my grandmother. She lived a mile from us. Again, Mama was up, movin' around when Grandma came. A lot of the time, she'd get up like that, but she'd talk things that didn't make sense. She'd go ahead, washin' dishes or preparin' a meal, and then in an hour or so she'd say, "Did I have one of those spells?" And she'd get terrific headaches afterwards.

We never knew about putting something between her teeth until I was pract'ly grown. A doctor told Dad to put a pencil or something. She used to chew her tongue so bad. She never did swallow her tongue. She would struggle so hard. It's a terrible thing to see. . . .

One time a sheep shearer's wife was here with her husband when they were shearing our sheep. She's from down in Idaho someplace, and she said her mother had seizures and she took this medication. She sent Mama some of these pills. Mama took 'em, and there was about a year that she didn't have a seizure. Whether we lost track of where this woman was, or where the pills come from in Idaho, I don't know. As she got older, Mama didn't have nearly as many seizures as she did when us kids were little. It seemed like if something worried her bad, it could bring on a seizure.

When Dad was gone, which he was a lot, I never slept sound. I'd be half awake all night for fear Mom'd go into one of those seizures. They make a sound that's not like any other. I'd beat it downstairs. To this day, I guess that's why I'm such a poor sleeper.

Community gatherings and dances were some of the most vivid memories Helen had of her childhood.

In the summertime, on the Fourth of July, ever'body in the vicinity tried to get together. They'd go in their wagons for a fish fry at the river. The women would bake and bake the day before, make all kinds of sandwiches, cakes and desserts, and potato salad.

I remember this one time Mama and Miz Myrtle Dorval each had babies in their arms, and we'd driven up out of a draw where Indian Crick overflowed sometimes. The men, Dad and Will, had the high seat in the front, Mama and Myrtle the high seat in the back. Us kids were all in the bottom. As the wagon come up out of the draw, Mama and Myrtle were both nursin' their babies. The seat come off the wagon, and down went Mama and Myrtle into the crick bed. I can still remember Myrtle yellin', "Wool," she never said Will, "Wool, you killed us, you killed us!" They were pretty battered up, but neither of the babies were hurt a bit.

Never firecrackers on the Fourth of July. For entertainment, one of my uncles and one of the Pierson boys'd have a horse race. These two guys, race down the road for a mile, maybe half a mile. It seems a long ways when you're a kid.

I remember one picnic we went to, up on Wolf Crick, and it was a hot day. When I think of it now, little girls going on a picnic, little white all-embroidered dress, a little old hat that sat on the top of your head that was no shade at all. I had long curls, a big ribbon bow half as big as my head. I had never seen Indian paintbrushes and there was lots of them up there. They looked so bright and red, I had more fun runnin' around pickin' them. I got so sunburned that day, by the time we got home I was blisterin'. I stayed at my grandmother's, and she kept puttin' sweet cream on my aunt and I, we were burnin' so. When the cream would get warm on your sunburn, it would smell like a cow barn.

When I was real small, there was a grocery store at Cameron, six miles from us. They had groceries and dry goods. You could buy dress material, thread, stuff like that. The first dance I can remember, we went down there. They had it above the store. I thought my Aunt Pearl was the most beautiful woman I ever saw. She had on such a pretty blue dress with a real high neck. Of course, they all wore long dresses then. She was a thin person and had lots of black hair. I was so happy that she was my aunt!

Somebody played the organ, and somebody played the violin. That's what they did for most dances when I was a kid. Later, they'd take turns havin' dances in their homes. There was a man and a lady that lived up on Wolf Crick from us; she would second on the organ and he would fiddle. They went ever'place to dances and played for them.

We never had a babysitter in our life. We always went. When the kids got sleepy, they laid them on the bed, as many as would fit, covered 'em up with coats and they'd sleep 'til the dance was over. I was so fascinated I didn't sleep much.

Sometimes we'd lie down for an hour or two, but then we got up and went right to work. When I got older, we'd come home and get the cows milked and have breakfast and go right on gettin' the next meal ready and not go to bed at all. Those cows had to be milked. The hired men didn't go to the dances. You had to be sure to have your meals on time for them.

In those days, if you had a day off when you didn't have a bunch of men to cook for, you went to a neighbor's for the day. You took your darning or patchwork, somethin' to do. You didn't have an invitation to come. We never was invited. We just went. Or a neighbor, she had a day off, she'd bring all her kids and her darning. Socks they did, or patchin' overalls. You could always get up a good dinner: meat and potatoes and gravy, a vegetable, a dessert. We would have such a good visit!

We used to go, maybe once during the summer, to Piersons'. I think that was close to a four-mile walk. Mama would have to carry my youngest brother piggy-back some, because he would play out. We would take a lunch with us. When we got hungry, Mama would set down with us. We'd eat a little lunch, and then we'd go on. We would stay a day or two with Mrs. Pierson. She had a big family, and she never got away from home much. A wonderful person. She was a schoolteacher, and she was such an interesting person to visit. Ever'place else we always walked to and came back the same day.

We had lots of closer neighbors than that. When we lived at the homestead, it was just about a mile to Grandma's and Grandpa's, and it wasn't quite a mile to Uncle Virge and Aunt Blythe. The Johnsons [name changed] lived about a mile and a half, the Herndons about a mile and a half. The Armitages was close to three miles. The Johnson family we visited with a lot, because they were neighbors to my Granddad Carkeek. I don't think they would have survived if it hadn't been for the food Grandpa gave them. I can remember Pearl comin' up in the old wagon with all these kids. They had a big family, seven or eight children. She would come early in the morning and they would stay and have dinner, and then they would stay and have supper with us. When she got ready to go home, she'd say, "Lily, can I borrow a sack of flour? I haven't got any flour in my house."

Dad and his brothers would usually kill a deer or two extry in the fall to give to the Johnsons so they'd have meat. I don't know why Horace never seemed to work much. I can still remember those kids, they just amazed us, the way they ate. They didn't have much food.

The Johnsons milked a lot of cows. That's one thing they had, lots of milk. And butter and cream. I s'pose for breakfast they never had much but cereal. I think they had a few chickens. They were hard up. We visited back and forth with them a lot. Pearl would always fix us a pretty good tastin' dinner with creamed potatoes and a few things. You never went away hungry.

In the wintertime, there were maybe five months that we would never go to town. And in the summer, I'd say we went three or four times. We were on the ranch, and that's where we stayed.

I s'pose Dad went to town maybe once a week, sometimes once in two weeks. The bank was in Ennis, and he had to come down on banking business a lot. He always brought groceries when he come home. In the summertime we couldn't keep fresh meat, so those times Dad would come home late in the evening and bring a big roast or boiling beef. We'd have a boil of beef with Mama's homemade noodles. It wasn't a treat to have chicken and noodles, 'cause we had our own chickens.

When Helen's father went to town, he drove a team and wagon in the summer and a sled in the winter. On at least one occasion, however, the family enjoyed a more elegant conveyance.

The first time I remember comin' to Ennis, we came with a neighbor who had a big touring car. It took us all day to come that twenty-five miles. We stayed over one or two days at the Fitzgerald Hotel. I thought it was quite exciting to stay in a room in a hotel and to sit down to eat with all those people you didn't know.

The food was served family style, just what they had prepared. Plenty of it. I guess maybe they inquired how many was goin' to eat. There was a big long table, lots of people that ate, but we didn't know anybody but Mrs. Fitzgerald.

Then, when we went home, I don't know how many flat tires we had, but it took us all day to go back. To get down in the bowl where we lived, you had to go up a little hill, and this man didn't think his car would make it. We got to his place, which was over the hill north from us, just about dusk. We had to walk from there over to our place in the dark.

We had such a few things to play with, few things to do, but I can't remember ever getting bored. I hear kids say, "What shall I do?" I could always think of something to do. I could spend hours playin' with dolls. The paper dolls I had were people cut out of catalogs. I'd string Dad and Mom's trunks with people and furniture and play with those things for days. We had one neighbor that got *McCall's Magazine* that had this Dolly Dimple paper doll in it. She would bring that magazine over for me to cut the paper dolls out. I thought it was the most wonderful thing, to have a real paper doll that you could put a dress or a coat on.

The boys, they amused themselves playin' marbles a lot. Didn't have very many, but they liked to play marbles. As children, we never ever had very many toys.

We had no telephone; we didn't even have a Victrola. When I was fourteen or fifteen, Dad got a radio. I'd been married two or three years when I finally saved up enough money and bought a little Victrola for twelve dollars.

Children today have too much. I've got grandkids that make me sick when I see all the stuff they have and the money put into them. Like these little horses they have with the colored manes and tails. I think my granddaughter's got maybe fifteen of those, and they cost better than five dollars apiece. And she's got the pony palace and the shower and everything that goes with those ponies. She don't give a darn about a doll, but she loves those horses.

Helen's clearest memories were often of simple pleasures, such as a much-loved poem from her school days.

I always thought Longfellow's poems were pretty. I loved "Evangeline." The words were so beautiful. There was a girl in the eighth grade when I was in sixth or seventh. When she would read "Evangeline," I wouldn't study. I'd stick a book up like this [pretending to read], but all the time I was listening to her.

I'd love to get ahold of one of those old red-back eighth-grade readers to have that poem. One of the teachers here gave me two books of "Evangeline," but the words don't seem the same as they were in that old red reader.

Helen met her husband, Denny Wonder, when she was only seventeen. They married eight months later and spent their honeymoon camping in the mountains while Denny trapped bears for the government.

I was never really engaged. I just got married when I was seventeen, much against my mother's wishes. Dad introduced me to Denny at a cafe in Ennis. He was a government trapper. Dad said, "This man's going to live in the Cox house [a house owned by the Clarks] for the winter and trap coyotes."

Denny was a World War I veteran. He was gassed with mustard gas. After the war, he spent two years at Battle Mountain Sanitarium in Hot Springs, South Dakota. They were going to put him in the TB ward. He knew he didn't have TB, so he checked himself out of the sanitarium and come out to the Bitterroot Valley [Montana]. He went into a logging camp, sawmill, it was. He asked them for a job and the first thing the boss says, "You look like you oughta be in the hospital." Denny said, "I just got out of two years in the hospital." The fella said, "Stick around, we're gonna have dinner pretty soon." In the afternoon he said, "If you're not too tired, you might split a little wood or chore a little for the cook." That's the way he started in. Then he went to work for the Forest Service. For several years he worked for the Forest Service in the summertime and trapped in the winter. He lived outdoors all year round, and he got his health back.

Then he heard about this government hunting job [a program aimed at protecting domestic sheep from marauding bears]. He put in for it.

We met in September, and we were married the next May. My mother was against it. Dad said, "Well, if you want to get married, you might as well get married." My grandmother said, "They could get the justice of the peace to marry them." Dad said, "No, they'll be married in the Episcopal church at Jeffers." Dad was very anti-preacher, didn't believe—he said all the heaven and hell you have, you have on earth—but he always swore that you had to be married and buried from the church. My mother said if you weren't married in the church, you weren't married. Justice of the peace, she didn't consider you married at all.

One of my aunts and an uncle stood up with us. I was seventeen, he was thirty-three. Everybody knew it wouldn't last a year. It lasted 'til he died in 1965. To this day, people have asked me why I didn't marry again. I've never seen anybody who could fit his shoes. I'd rather be alone.

We spent our honeymoon back in the mountains. Denny was hunting bear for the government. The mountains here were full of sheep, so many different sheep companies in the valley at that time.

I'll always cherish the memories of that first summer. We were married in May, we went into the mountains the seventh of July, and we didn't come out 'til September when we come out with the sheep.

We had a new twelve-by-four tent, which we were really proud of. Denny built up a nice bed of fir boughs, which were kind of springy. He built a bed and put little poles up from the bottom of it to help hold in the boughs. It was a pretty good bed. He built a table and a bench out of poles. We were very comfortable.

We had a little tin cookstove. I think it cost all of five dollars. It was prob'ly thirty inches long and eighteen inches wide. The oven was out from the box you put the wood in. It could get awful hot with that firebox along one side of it. You fed the wood through a door. Most of the time, if you baked anything, you had to leave the oven door open or it burned. We cut down some willows, set it on four legs.

Things take so long to cook in the mountains. Some of the camps we were in, the elevation was eight, nine thousand feet. In fact, the Sphinx is ten thousand feet, and we did have one camp that was way up on the side of the Sphinx. You could boil dry beans for a day and a half before they would be edible. Potatoes and meat, which is your staple food, cooked fine. It just took longer. I made pies and a few plain cakes. I never tried bakin' bread, but I made biscuits, muffins, stuff like that.

I usually went with Denny on the trapline; I cooked and did laundry. Dad was tendin' his own sheep camp, so he stayed a lot at our camp. I kept busy.

Some days, if I had laundry or something to do, I stayed in camp and Denny went alone to check the traps. I took a lot of embroidery to do. I said to Mama, "Every time Dad comes into camp, send me a lot of stuff to read." She never did, except for a few newspapers. I embroidered a lunch cloth, one little butterfly all summer. Didn't have time! Too many things to do, especially when you rode every day.

To do laundry, we took a washtub and a washboard in with us. We heated the water on the camp stove. With only one tub, you washed everything in the soapy water, then wrung it out, dipped water out of the crick, rinsed two or three times. We hung the clothes to dry on a line we strung up. We wore everything unironed.

We always got up early. We'd be on the trail by 5, 5:30, especially when the horseflies got so bad. You had to check with the sheepherders to see if they were havin' any trouble. It required a lot of riding. Then maybe we'd come in at 3 or 4 in the afternoon when the flies were so bad. Denny made high posters on the bed. We had a big mosquito netting we could drift over our bed and get out of the flies.

We'd have to ride down to the Gallatin River for Denny to mail out his reports. It was called the Eldridge Post Office then, the 320 Dude Ranch now. It was quite a long ride. We had to go up over the Cinnamon Mountain, which was up and down, steep on the other side. Then you rode from the ranger station to the post office, another couple of miles. Once, when we come out to mail the report, a bear visited our tent. We had it tied to a big fir tree, and we had ham and bacon up the tree. The bear climbed up, got on the ridgepole of the tent and fell through the tent and tore it, then went out through another corner. One side of the tent was demolished. Sure ruined our tent we were so proud of. A lot of our food, too. It got the ham and the bacon; it bit a lot of the cans and ruined canned goods, too. We didn't have much love for bears that summer.

I don't think I ever had a greater sense of freedom than I had that summer. It was such a beautiful summer. It was kind of sad, leavin' the mountains when it was over. When you're your own boss, you can do as you please. Denny was workin' for the government and had to take care of the bear situation; still, you were free to get up and go when you wanted, work as long as you wanted to. And some days were very long, especially when he got a bear. He had to skin 'em out even though the hides were no good. And skin the feet down to the toes . . . a tedious job. Skin out the head, send in the skull. Denny would find an anthill and put the head on it, and the ants would clean the meat off it. The hides would have to be pegged down on the ground and the fat taken off, salted real heavy with sheep salt, leave 'em 'til they dried. He also had to cut the stomachs open to see if they had wool in 'em, check to see if there was wool in the teeth, see what the bear had been feeding on. Never killed a one that didn't have sheep wool in its stomach.

So many people were in sympathy with the bear. I'll admit it wasn't right to leave it for an hour, dying, but when you see twenty-eight sheep that's been killed in one night by bear, and a half dozen more with a leg tore half off, or tore up so that you had to destroy 'em, you don't have much love for a bear.

After their summer in the mountains, the newlyweds lived for a time on the Clark ranch.

Denny was workin' and irrigatin' for Dad on the ranch. We stayed on there, and he took up a homestead on Indian Crick, eighty acres. He did the first clearin' the brush off of it the day our first daughter was born.

When she was five months old, he got out logs and built a log house. We lived there for seven years and had two more daughters.

When we lived up Indian Crick, my husband was sick a lot and couldn't work, but he was given thirty-two dollars a month pension, which we did all right on. Then when Roosevelt went in, the first thing he did was cut all the veterans' pensions. It was cut to $15.32. That's what we had to live on with a baby on the way. You had to figure out which month you could buy a few yards of outing flannel to make some diapers. It depended on how the food [supply] was.

I baked bread and sold to some bachelors up there, twenty-five cents a loaf. They were big loaves, prob'ly weighed two, two and a half pounds.

We had to eat deer and fish and live pretty much off the land. When you kill deer in the wintertime and they're feedin' on sagebrush . . . I thought I never wanted to see another piece of deer meat.

Serviceberries I never did like very good, but you could pick chokecherries and mix them with serviceberries and it helped both. Pit as you might, it took an hour to pit a quart of chokecherries! But still, I'd love right now to have a piece of chokecherry pie. Chokecherry's my favorite jelly. I also like wild gooseberries. I don't think tame gooseberries can compare with the flavor the wild gooseberry has.

When we lived on the homestead up Indian Crick, we could raise the most wonderful heads of lettuce because the nights up there were cold and the heads would crisp up. We had so much, we give it to ever'body that would have a head of it. We had LOTS of lettuce, and we had lots of it go to waste.

We tried to have chickens, but the hawks always got 'em. We had a cow for one summer. One of the neighbors give us a cow to milk, but it got to where I'd have to walk up the canyon a mile to milk the cow. That got to be too much of a chore. And we'd have to buy hay in the winter, so we just turned her back.

We used to buy milk from a neighbor. They milked several cows. I'd get half a gallon to have milk for the kids to drink. She charged me fifteen cents for it. It was hard times. One morning we said to Clarice, our oldest daughter, "What do you want for breakfast?" She said, "Tatahs and beans." We often had potatoes but never had beans for breakfast.

I did a lot of cryin' the summer I was pregnant with Catherine, when we were so hard up. I was always a worrywart, and I was worryin' how we were going to feed another child. We were having such a struggle with just one, and him not bein' able to work much of the time. Wages didn't amount to nothing, either. A good man might make thirty, thirty-five dollars a month. That was it. He could never work steady like that. He was a person that would rather go help somebody out for a day or two than to work for wages. He did that a lot. Which was a good thing, but sometimes it was too good a thing for your own benefit.

We would buy our sugar and flour and shortening. We would get lard from the pig we'd buy. It was never enough to put us through. In the fall of the year, we would lay in enough sugar and flour and coffee. At that time, I never drank coffee and Denny didn't drink very much. When you get down to fifteen dollars a month, you set down for a week and figure . . . do I have to have soda this month or can I put it off 'til next month, because I need baking powder worse this month. You had to figure out what you *had* to have.

I canned lots of fish. My husband didn't have the patience to do much fishing, but we had a neighbor, a disabled veteran, who went fishing practically ever' day. He'd bring us big rainbow or Loch Leven trout, and I'd can 'em up. Put a little salt and olive oil in 'em.

One time when Uncle Frank come out from Butte, he brought eight people with him. When you don't have much to live on and you have that many people drop in on you, what in the world will you feed 'em? I'll give 'em some fish. Aunt Winnie wouldn't touch it, but Uncle Frank said he never tasted salmon as good as that fish.

My aunt said, "I don't know how you do it. If you come to Butte, I couldn't give you bread and butter and coffee without goin' to the store for one or all three items. Here I bring eight in on you and you can fix something to eat." I probably hadn't been to the store in a month.

People don't hardly believe me when I tell 'em there would be five months at a time in the winter when I'd never come to town. The snow was a lot worse in those years than it is now. Althouse [a neighbor] had a big truck. Denny would go down to Althouses, and they'd come to town together . . . cut across the flats and find their way around the snowdrifts. They'd get a month's supply of groceries. The women didn't go to town.

I don't think I ever got lonesome or wished I was out of there until my second daughter had convulsions. At the time we didn't have a car. We had to get a neighbor to bring us to a doctor. Then I wished we didn't live there. But otherwise I kept busy 'til I never got lonesome. We didn't have a telephone or radio. My dad and some of the neighbors had them. You didn't get any reception until night. We used to walk down to this old bachelor's place on Saturday night to hear the square dancin' from Calgary.

We never did have a phone or a radio up there. We finally bought a beautiful old Victrola off of people who were neighbors from the time I was born. They moved to Butte, and she wanted to get rid of the Victrola. Not a scratch on it, a beautiful piece of furniture. And she had lots of records, those big thick records. "Helen," she said, "I'll sell you that for twenty-five dollars."

I used to play that thing all day long when Denny was gone. Of course, it didn't change records like these modern ones do, and you had to keep cranking it up. But, oh, I enjoyed it so much. There were nice old songs like "I'll Take You Home Again, Kathleen" and pretty songs, "Memories" and "Lay My Head beneath the Rose." People today would laugh at them, but they were beautiful old songs, beautiful singing. There was so much meaning to the words in the songs then. In the first and second grades at school, I learned all those old songs, "Old Black Joe," "My Old Kentucky Home."

There was a lot of sad times; you spent a lot of time cryin', wonderin' how you was goin' to manage to get along on such a little. You and your husband would talk things over and decide what you had to get along on, what you could do and that was it. It made a marriage stronger, I'm sure it did.

Life was pretty simple. In the wintertime we had a 500 party with six or seven neighbors. Ever' two weeks we'd go to somebody's house and play 500 'til midnight. They always took a moonlight night to come to our place because they'd have to come up in sleds. It was so beautiful there in the canyon in the moonlight.

You'd have refreshments and coffee, sandwiches and cake, all you could eat, at midnight or whenever they quit playin' cards. If the roads was kinda bad, we wouldn't come home 'til it was gettin' daylight. We never had babysitters. The kids were always brought and put to bed crossways and covered with coats.

It was a lot of fun. People enjoyed their neighbors to where now people don't. You don't get together; you don't do things together. A few of us do, once in a while. We used to, me and a couple of neighbors, have coffee at ten o'clock ever' morning. One neighbor moved away, and the other and I have coffee together once in a while.

I think people are less neighborly now because of the boob tube. We always, when somebody comes, shut the television off. But I've been to so many places, they *will not shut that television off.* You can't talk above the thing, so you stay a little bit and go home. When you didn't have television, you sat down and had a good visit.

Helen learned to use a gun at a young age and continued to hunt throughout her life.

Dad used to let us kids take the .22 and shoot gophers. I'd take the .22 and shoot gophers on the way to and from the mailbox, a quarter of a mile from home. That's all I ever shot. Then that summer we were married and lived back in the mountains, Denny got me to practice up. He was a crack shot and a gun collector. The first thing I killed with a rifle was a woodchuck, and I killed a bear. I laid off hunting for several years, and then my husband got so bad, he couldn't go alone anymore. I went with him, and whichever one of us got a chance to shoot, we shot, so we always had meat. I've kept it up ever since.

I had a cousin who was a widow woman, and her and I hunted a lot together. She died, and for five years I didn't hunt. I didn't even know where my rifle was. Then, once when I was up to Cut Bank, Greg, my grandson, said, "Granny, I've got your rifle." I said, "I've been tryin' to find it for the last four years." He put a good scope on it, and now he takes me hunting.

I don't shoot 'til I'm pretty sure of my shot. I shot a .243. It's got a lot of killin' power, but it's not long range. I don't shoot to wound. There was eight years that I had a perfect score. I fired eight shots and got eight deer.

After their years on the Clark ranch, Helen and Denny moved to the town of Jeffers, where Helen lived on long after becoming a widow.

Jeffers is a good place to raise kids. My yard has always been full of kids and is yet. Never havin' had a saloon here, Jeffers never grew. I think that's the reason ...never allowed a saloon. This property doesn't have it, but the houses across the street, all up and down, it's in their deeds, if they ever sell liquor, the property reverts to the heirs of the original Jeffers family.

We have wonderful neighbors. They're good to help each other out. If you're in trouble, everybody pitches in to help you.

Wasn't many big things ever happened. It was lots of little things, which are nice to reminisce on now.

Helen Wonder was interviewed at her home in Jeffers in March 1987. She died there in August 2002. She was ninety-one years old.

MADGE SWITZER WALKER

*"My goodness, what do we know
about hard times?"*

Madge Switzer Walker was born in Jeffers, Montana, on September 10, 1891, the child of Carrie and Tavner Switzer. Her paternal grandparents were early pioneers who settled in the Madison Valley in 1865, one year after the region was organized as Montana Territory and twenty-four years before Montana entered the union as the forty-first state.

Madge's Grandmother Switzer, as well as Madge's mother, believed emphatically in education for women. In 1914, Madge Switzer received her degree in home economics from Montana Agricultural College, known today as Montana State University. She remained interested in ideas well into her nineties, when she was still an active member of a local book club.

Before her marriage to Eric Walker, she worked for several years, first as a dietician at St. Peter's Hospital in Helena, then as head of the home economics department at Bozeman (Montana) High School.

My grandparents, Andrew and Elizabeth Switzer, came from Victor, Iowa. That's in Poweshiek County, in the southeastern corner of the state. They started with four oxen and three covered wagons. Grandpa Switzer had one wagon. Malpheus Switzer, Grandpa's brother, rode horseback along beside them. Law [another relative] had the second wagon. I can't remember about the third wagon. . . .

They left Iowa the first of May 1865, and they got to Virginia City September 30. That was . . . five months.

Grandma had a girl, ten, and a girl, eight. My dad was a year and a half, and she had a six-week-old baby. She was afraid to go into a dark room. Think what she must have suffered; it must have been terrible. And she didn't want to come! When they left Iowa, she went over to the railroad, a little ways from their farm, and rode for seven miles. I think she thought that would be the last time she'd ever see a railroad.

When they got to the Platte River, she and Aunt Ellen cut their hair off. They had long hair, and it was just too much trouble, so they cut it off and laid it across a stump. They said, "Now they'll think we've been scalped!"

Grandma Switzer told me a story about an Indian. Nez Perce were coming through the valley. They had their women and children with them, but this young fellow came to her house. It was a one-room cabin, with one window, one door, and she was outside washing on the board in the tub. The Indian—she was afraid of him—took out his knife. The children were crying; she was afraid she was going to be scalped. He sharpened the knife on a rock, then he pulled a hair out of his head and cut it to see if it was sharp. Now she was really scared! I said, "What did you do?" And she said, "I washed as hard as I could wash."

The Indian took a turnip out of his pocket and peeled it!

She thought how foolish she was to have been afraid. The Nez Perce were traveling with their women and children; they wouldn't be on the warpath, and they wouldn't be up to any mischief. She was just so frightened, and she had those little children. . . .

I think the women that came west had more . . . shall I say *guts*, and then it'll be there, than any women nowadays. My goodness, what do we know about hard times?

After the first year [1865–66] in the one-room cabin, Grandpa Jeffers [actually the grandfather of Walker's cousins] got out logs and he took up a homestead near the present town of Jeffers. Later [1871], my Uncle Myron Jeffers bought the Yellow Barn Cattle Ranch nearby.

When they wanted a post office there [1903], Myron's widow [Florence Switzer Jeffers] was instrumental in having it named Jeffers. How much she had to do 'bout it, I don't know, but she was a woman who did things like that.

Grandpa Switzer had a herd of purebred Brown Swiss cows, the first in the valley. He milked, oh, maybe about a dozen cows. I don't think Grandma ever went out to milk; he brought the milk in. She put it in pans, tin pans about that big around [indicates a sizable pan]. He'd built her a rack that let these pans fit in. She'd leave the milk 'til the next day, and then she'd take the cream off the top. By that time it was stiff; you could almost lift it up. She skimmed the cream and made butter; she used the skim milk to make cottage cheese.

Grandma made butter in a barrel churn. That's the kind that goes around and turns over. She turned it with a handle, over and over. There was a little glass window in the barrel churn [to check the progress of the butter]. When the butter commenced to come, it seems to me she put in some water—warm water—kind of hurried it up. She put her butter in two-pound wooden molds and sold it for twenty-five cents a pound.

To make cottage cheese, she put the milk on the back of the stove in a fair-sized vessel, a kettle, and left it there overnight. By morning it would have clabbered. Then she put it in a cheesecloth bag and drained it. My Grandmother Pickens always made her cottage cheese into balls, twice as big as a golf ball. Then she rolled them in caraway seeds, and I can't stand caraway seeds to this day! The cheese was good, except that nowadays we get a soft curd. That was a hard curd, and it was much smaller. They always used skim milk because the cream was valuable for butter.

Later on, they got a separator, and that was quite a something. We would have that separated cream on fresh currants. The cream was, oh, it was too rich!

The separator was an innovation. It was an iron rack, and there was a bowl at the top of it with discs that dipped into the bowl. You'd crank until you got it to the point where it didn't whine. You could tell by the sound of it if you were going fast enough. It separated the cream from the milk. Centrifugal, you see. The cream went to the outside, the skim milk went to the inside. There were two spouts, one for the skim milk, one for the cream. And the cream, it could be adjusted—I haven't thought of these things for so long—it could be adjusted so the cream was very thick or very thin.

I can't remember ever seeing Grandma Switzer wash the separator, but I can remember when *I* washed the separator. And I hated it! I think it was more because everybody said, "Oh, the separator is so bad!" There was so much talk, I thought I should dislike it, too. There were twenty-four of those discs, and they were awkward to handle, and, well, you just didn't like to do it. It was like cleaning up the lamps in the morning. You had to do that. You had to put the kerosene in, trim the wick, and wash the chimney. And that's one of the first things you did if you were a good housekeeper.

I know that as soon as my Grandmother Switzer got into the valley, she was bound there was going to be a school. There had to be a school, and there had to be a church. Grandma Switzer was a persevering woman. She raised chickens, sold cottage cheese, butter, and eggs. She put her girls through school, a school for young ladies in Virginia City. She didn't bother about the boy. My dad probably went to school six months in his life, but he was a pretty smart man.

I remember once—I was just a little thing—going down to Grandma Switzer's house. When I got there, she had taken baby chickens away from a setting hen. She had them in a basket, and she let me look at them. Oh, they were cunning, just little puffs. I covered them up carefully, too carefully. When she uncovered them, they were all dead. Those chickens meant something to her; they were dollars and cents. As well as being sorry for the chickens. But she didn't scold me; she didn't say a word.

At Grandma Switzer's they didn't eat in the kitchen. They had a dining room [this was a large house, built after the one-room log cabin], and sometimes they didn't have enough chairs to go around, so they sat on boxes and tree stumps. Her kitchen had a woodstove with a reservoir in the back and a big oven. She made loaves and *loaves* and LOAVES of bread. And cookies—she made lots of cookies in the fall when she had eggs and butter and cream. They were raised sugar cookies, about two inches across, and they puffed up in the middle. She put them in a barrel, and they lasted through the winter.

Madge grew up surrounded by a large, interconnected family that included two sets of grandparents, Marilla and Benjamin Pickens and Elizabeth and Andrew Switzer; numerous aunts and uncles; and a number of double cousins.

My Grandmother Pickens on my mother's side was a Jeffers. Two Jeffers men, Myron and Burton, came west and married two Switzer girls, Florence and Susie. And Mama married the Switzer boy. Mama and Papa were married in '88. It's quite a complicated, close-knit family.

Grandpa Switzer was a carpenter. He made a chest with bins that tilted out. Then there was a drawer where Grandma kept oatmeal; they bought oatmeal in hundred-pound sacks. The bins that had flour and sugar were in the kitchen, and on the top of them she had workspace. There was a cupboard for spices, a cupboard for dishes, too. The dishes were white with a brown design. There was a brown linoleum on the floor, and it was wiped up every day. *Every day.*

We used to come in through the pump house. It was a room built on the back of the kitchen. When people came through this pump house—it was about fifteen feet long, maybe ten feet wide—they were supposed to shed their overshoes and so on and so forth out there.

Grandma churned in the pump house. She made butter there because it was close to the well. The pump was not a pitcher pump, but one they had before pitcher pumps [hand-operated pumps for shallow wells].

Their winter kitchen was on the ground floor, then you went down several steps and there was the summer kitchen. They cooked down there in warm weather. I remember there was a little crick that ran under that summer kitchen. I think they dipped the water that they drank out of there. I think they washed down there, too, did their laundry.

My early schooling was at the Maynard School, close to my grandfather's homestead. I walked, well, maybe it was a mile north, and I had some cousins—they were the Burt Jeffers children—that lived a half a mile south of us. They'd stop in the morning and pick me up. I remember I had a coat, big sleeves, long, and a tie, a silk tie that was very pretty. I wonder where that coat is? You don't suppose I threw it away? I hope I didn't. I'll have to look for it.

I remember we had a smallpox scare. The teacher had vaccine, and he'd been instructed how to give these smallpox vaccinations. He'd come and stay all night, and everybody in the family got a vaccination. I got mine, and it never bothered me a bit, but my sister had an awful time. Her whole arm was swelled; I had a little scab. I was tough.

Speaking of the Maynard School prompted Madge's recollection of a humorous incident involving a teacher there many years later.

Eric [Madge's husband] worked for the Hudson Sheep Company. They kept their sheep on Grandpa Switzer's place. They kept their bucks separate, about forty of them. Eric fed 'em oats from a tobacco can, one with the lid that came over the top. And one day the teacher, who lived at Aunt Ellen's place, was going to the Maynard School, comin' down the lane with her lunch in a box just like that. The bucks thought it was their dinner, and they pert near swamped her, nearly scared her to death.

There was a store in Jeffers—I couldn't have been more than . . . I must have been about six. I can remember a barrel of gingersnaps, and I can remember a knife that cut plug tobacco. I remember a wheel of cheese, and it was covered with a glass cover; there was a knife that worked on a pivot from the inside, and you cut a wedge of cheese.

Sugar was sold out of cloth bags, flour and oatmeal, too. Coffee, I remember, came in paper bags. Arbuckles.

Have you been in Virginia City where they have the drawers with the glass in front? It shows what it is: beans and peas, stuff like that. He had one of those. Oyster crackers in this barrel, another barrel had dill pickles. You just dipped in and got you some pickles. And this barrel that had gingersnaps: It was open to the public and to the flies! How did we live? And we thrived!

And then on the other side of the store was dry goods. They had bolts of cloth and needles and pins and thread and maybe some lace.

Uncle John worked as a clerk in the store. He and Aunt May lived in the back of the store. I think the post office was back there, too.

Saunders's meat wagon came around once a week. He'd let down a door in the back, and there were scales that came out. You got what you wanted, and he cut it right there. He had baloney and beef.

I remember going to Virginia City one time. We had one horse and a buggy. It was Nell that we drove; she was a gray mare. My mother and my grandmother were there, just the three of us.

Grandma Pickens was quite a hand to sing, and they sang "Fling Out the Banner Far and Wide." I sat in the bottom of the buggy, right at their feet. We started early in the morning, and we didn't get home until late at night....

We bought a rockin' chair for me, and where that rockin' chair went ... [wistfully] ... I don't know....

Madge Walker was interviewed in her apartment in Pray, Montana, in November 1982. She died in Livingston in December 1989. She was ninety-eight years old.

MARIE WALKER CONVERSE

"When I think back, I wonder,
how did I do all that?"

Marie Walker Converse was born in Hillsdale, Illinois, on August 14, 1897. She was a tiny, attractive, gregarious woman, with a beautiful smile. She claimed that she wouldn't have ended up in Montana if it hadn't been for her father's dreams. Daniel Walker was a butcher by trade; his wife was a homemaker.

My father fell in love with Montana when he came out here in 1897, the year I was born. He came back home, but he wasn't satisfied until he was able to make the move to Montana.

We came in March of 1904, traveling by train. We brought our household things and farm machinery in an emigrant car. We had a sleeper; Mother and I slept in the lower berth, Father and my brother slept in the upper berth.

I was always watching when they lit the coal-oil lamps on the train. They were up on the side, and the brakeman would come through at a certain time at night to light each one.

We were to come to Harlowton, which was a division point [on the railroad]. From there we were to take what they called the Jawbone Railroad [officially known as the Montana Central] to Lewistown. When we got to Harlowton, there was so much snow on the ground, the Jawbone was closed, so we went on to Lombard. There was a big hotel there run by a Chinese family. The hotel was full, with so many people coming from Illinois and central Missouri and Nebraska, all stranded by the snow. We stayed there about a week. I imagine my father was getting restless; we came on to Great Falls by train, and from Great Falls by stagecoach to Lewistown.

[The stagecoach] was all enclosed. We sat in the back, and the two drivers were up on a high seat. There were four horses. It was March, it was cold, and there was lots of snow on the ground. [The drivers] had fur-lined gloves and fur-lined coats. The coach had fur robes. The horses would flounder around [in the snow], and we'd have to get out. The drivers would spread one of those fur robes on the ground, and we'd sit there, the four of us, Mother, Father, my brother, and I. We'd have another robe over our laps until they'd dug the horses out. Get back in, keep going. Ever so often there'd be a whiskey bottle thrown overboard on this side, and it wouldn't be too long before there'd be one go off the other side. These were the *drivers!* There were windows in the coach, and I could see. I was scared to death. I was old enough to know. I knew the effect of drinking. My folks knew I was frightened. "You're all right, Marie. Mother and Dad are here."

There were stops, but we never did stay overnight anywhere. We changed drivers and horses every so often. It took us three days and two nights to go from Great Falls to Lewistown [a distance of 105 miles].

By the time we got to Lewistown—we got there about one o'clock, the third day—oh, it was a real Montana Chinook! Water running everywhere, no pavements. The streets were *so* muddy. The stagecoach drove up in front of a hotel where we stayed for several days. My father had a cousin [in Lewistown], Dr. Beatty, and they invited us to come and stay at their place. My brother was sick; he'd had the measles before we left Illinois, and on the way he caught cold. We got to Lewistown the thirteenth of March, and my brother passed away on the thirteenth of April, just a month to the day.

The funeral was held in an upstairs room in a boardinghouse where the family lived temporarily.

Just the family and a few relatives of my father's were there. The hearse was driven with horses. It seemed the cemetery was miles out in the country, and now it's right in the city. It was so hard on my folks. Mother always said that money must grow on trees to go through the hardships they did.

Daniel Walker's father, Marie's grandfather, had previously come from Illinois up the Missouri River to Fort Benton in 1863, at the time of the Civil War.

He was in sympathy with the South but would have had to have fought with the North. He couldn't bring himself to do that. He was married and had a daughter. Maybe [leaving them] wasn't the proper thing to do, but he felt so strongly, that's what he did. When he got back [to Illinois], he never did find his wife or his daughter, any trace of them whatever.

And then he married my grandmother, and they had two boys and a girl: my father, Uncle Mansfield, and Aunt Mary.

Most people were coming for the homestead claims, but Marie's father never did use his homestead right. He rented a farm several miles out of Lewistown, where they lived for a year. In 1905 her Grandpa Walker came out and took up a homestead in the Cottonwood Valley.

We moved over with Grandpa and lived on his homestead for a year or two until they proved up. In the meantime, Grandpa bought a bigger place, still up there on Cottonwood. His folks had died and left him a small amount of money. It's beautiful country in the foothills of the Snowy Mountains where we lived. I was up there not too many years ago. The roads are just the same. Now and then there's a new house, but the majority of those old houses are still there. People are still living in them. I recognized all those old places.

The snow gets so deep up there on Cottonwood. We didn't get to town all winter long, but now and then we'd go to visit neighbors with a bobsleigh and team. After we stocked up on groceries in the fall, we wouldn't go to Lewistown 'til spring.

The folks bought flour in hundred-pound sacks; we never bought less than twenty-five pounds of sugar, beans in a twenty-five-pound sack. The only canned goods was tomatoes. Tomatoes by the case, those 2½-sized cans. We didn't have fresh fruit; we had all kinds of dried fruit that came in big wooden boxes: apples and peaches, and pears, apricots, raisins, and prunes. We bought soda crackers in wooden boxes, ten, fifteen pounds. And we always had a few cows. We had our own milk; we made our own butter. Mother baked bread, and she baked all our cookies and cake.

The men were the ones who read. We didn't have a daily newspaper, but they stocked up on reading material before winter set in. We had a telephone in Illinois. My father couldn't be without one, so he got the other farmers together and they built a line from the head of Cottonwood. They didn't connect with Lewistown; it was just between neighbors. I still remember our number: a long and two shorts. Party line! Everybody listened to everybody that was on that line. Curiosity was part of it, but that was the only way we knew what was going on. We had no other communications, no radio, no TV.

We did get mail once a week if we were able to get to the Jones Post Office, which was about halfway in the valley between Lower Cottonwood and Upper Cottonwood. There'd be weeks at a time that we didn't get to the Jones's house. The snow was often four feet deep up there in the foothills of the Snowy Mountains.

We had no conveniences, but that was our way of life. I think we were happier than people are today. I never heard the word *stress*. Later years, I didn't know what it was.

Another word I never heard: SEX! Why, my goodness, I'd been married years and years. [Sex] was a no-no; you didn't talk about those things. I don't know whether I approve of sex education in schools. To me it hasn't diminished teenage pregnancy any.

I know *I* wasn't prepared for my first menstrual period! I was nearly fourteen, but I was terrified. Mother had never told me one thing. The only thing she ever told me was that if I acted like a lady I wouldn't have any trouble, and the boys would respect me.

Marie's mother was determined that she go to school regularly—Mrs. Walker never did like the farm—and they moved into Lewistown in February 1910. A second child, Ruth, was born in August 1910. Because Marie's earlier schooling had been erratic, she was placed in a grade level with children younger than she.

I started in the fifth grade, in 5B. I didn't go to school very long until they promoted me to 5A. I was nearly twenty when I finished high school, but it didn't hurt me a bit. I think I got more out of high school than those graduating when they were sixteen, seventeen.

During her junior and senior years in high school, Marie worked part-time in the Lewistown telephone office. At the suggestion of her father's cousin, the county superintendent of schools, she took the teachers' exam in her junior year. She was issued a second-grade certificate, good for eighteen months.

I graduated from Fergus High June 14, 1917. I stayed at the telephone office, thrashing around in my mind whether I should teach or whether I should accept the [recently offered] managership of the telephone company in Hobson [a small town near Lewistown].

The latter part of August, I came down from the office to find two gentlemen in the waiting room.

"Miss Walker," they said. "We've been to the county superintendent's office, and we have come to ask you to teach at our school in Winnett."

I gave it a second's thought. "Okay, I'll take it." My folks had moved to Winnett; that had something to do with my decision. I left the telephone office immediately and went out to my country school. It was the Pilgrim School, about seven miles east of Winnett. I boarded with a lovely family by the name of Giroux. They had two boys, Edward and Louis. I still get a Christmas card from Edward. Every year. Now and then he calls me. Just to hear my voice, he says.

I had twenty-two children in my school at Winnett. There was mud all around the school, and I had one youngster who would *not* clean his shoes. In those days, the teacher was the janitor. I got in my own coal, built my fires, swept the floors, cleaned the blackboards. Every youngster brought his lunch. They came on horseback and in buggies.

Once a terrible storm came up; there were only two families who got to school that day. The Girouxes, my boarding place, was only a quarter of a mile away, but you couldn't begin to see the house. I said to the youngsters, "There's no possible way we can leave this schoolhouse tonight." The Giroux boys and I went out to the coal shed and got plenty of coal, enough wood to start the fire which we'd have to keep going all night.

I said, "We may get hungry, but we won't starve to death. We'll stay right here." About that time, here came Mr. Giroux, his face all snow and frost. He had brought a long rope. "We'll make it," he said. "There isn't so much snow but what I can see the grass, and we'll stay on the road."

The oldest boy, the Drew boy, took one end of the rope and I took the other. We all joined hands; I think there were five other youngsters, and we kept them between us. The remaining rope was tied around Mr. Giroux's waist, and he led us. Every one of us, going that quarter of a mile, had our faces frosted.

We had supper, then everyone stayed at Girouxes' that night. The next day the skies cleared, and some of the parents made it through to the Girouxes' house.

It's prairie country at Winnett, and, oh, the blizzards are terrible. Ground blizzards, too. It was the visibility, and it was bitter cold, really bitter cold.

I always went out on the school ground and played with the children. I had some boys who were taller than I. One boy, who was a little bit rowdy, was swearing [once]. Charlie Young grabbed that boy around the neck and threw him down on the ground. He said, "You're not swearing before my teacher!" After that, he was a pretty good kid. I never did have any real problems with my youngsters.

The first time the county superintendent came to visit, I was so nervous I picked up my pencil and broke it right in two. She must have given me a pretty good report. I never did apply for a school; I was always offered them. I enjoyed teaching, but it's nerve-racking. There were some days when everything would go so well, but there were other days that, oh dear, a lot of aggravation. . . .

I went home on Friday night and stayed 'til Monday morning with nearly all my youngsters. It was the custom at that time, the teacher had to come spend a weekend. The parents got to know me.

The [first] fall at the Pilgrim School, there was a going-away party at the Girouxes' house for two boys who were going into the service, Fred Newsome and Selah Converse. When the party broke up, Selah wanted to know if he could write to me. I said, "Yes," although I was going with a fellow in Lewistown. I thought it would be nice to have a letter from a soldier boy. We corresponded but not very regularly. He got one of my letters after he got home. After we were married!

When my first term was out, I had to renew my certificate. I went to summer school in Lewistown, and after the exam I got a first-grade certificate.

I taught two years at the Pilgrim School. The second summer I went to a little school at Arrow Crick. Of those youngsters, only one could speak a word of English. The rest of the children were from a Finnish family.

I had no special material to work with; I had to make my own. I stayed up at nights cutting pictures out of the Sears and Roebuck catalog, pasting them on cardboards. I'd have the picture and the word. I'd print it; I'd write it also. I had those youngsters reading and speaking English at the end of three months. They were doing real well, but because of the weather, they had school for just three months in the summer.

They were wonderful little children. When I first went there, they were so shy. Recess time or noon, I'd have to go out and round 'em up and bring 'em into the school. They got over that, and I really enjoyed those three months.

I taught reading, writing, arithmetic, geography, history. We had textbooks, but we had no teachers' guides. I did get a lot of information from one book that I bought somewhere, a book on how to teach.

My salary was seventy-five dollars a month. I paid thirty-five dollars a month for my room and board. It didn't leave me very much, but I didn't have the upkeep of a car, I had no insurance of any kind to pay. They took a dollar out of my paycheck [to be] put in the teachers' retirement fund.

The last part of August 1919, the county superintendent had a school for me at Moore. [A few months after] I went to Moore, I got a letter from this Selah Converse. He'd just been discharged from the service, from the Army of Occupation. He said he'd like to come out to see me.

We spent Thanksgiving with my folks in Winnett; then he went back to Minnesota and spent the rest of the winter with his folks. He came back in the spring. He had his homestead out there right close to the school. We were married in May of the next year, 1920.

The wedding was very, very simple. We went to the Methodist parsonage and were married in the living room. My aunt and uncle stood up with us as witnesses. Then we went to their house and had a supper. Selah had written an uncle at Winifred [Montana] and told them he was getting married. They came but didn't get there in time to go to the parsonage with us. They knew my aunt and uncle, so they came up to their house and spent the evening with us.

My parents didn't come. My mother hated to see me marry. I don't think it bothered my dad, but my mother was very disappointed that I didn't go on to school. I had fully intended to go on; I had a four-year scholarship to Bozeman [Montana Agricultural College]. Whenever I'd get a little provoked at Selah, I'd say, "I jumped from the frying pan into the fire."

My folks gave us a set of silver, Selah's father gave us a set of silver which I still have, and a couple of his aunts gave us a bedspread. The hardware man gave us a double boiler. Mrs. Giroux sent me a little colander and a set of muffin tins. I still have them. That was the sum and substance of our wedding gifts.

A lot of girls had hope chests. They had sheets, pillowcases, quilts, and everything else. I didn't have a hope chest, so we started out from scratch in the true sense.

Selah had 160 acres, a chance to buy 160 more, which made 320. After we were married, we bought two 40s which gave us 400 acres. He had his homestead shack [before he was drafted], and it was a *shack,* one thickness of boards nailed on the outside of the two-by-fours. Our cupboards were apple boxes; our washstand was an apple box, and it held a water pail with a dipper in it. The chimney was just a stovepipe up through a hole in the roof.

There was just one room. It had a homemade table and a store-bought bed. Selah had gone to an auction a few days before we were married and bought a cupboard, one of those that had glass doors with shelves down below and a piece up on top. When he got it home, it was too tall, so he set it outside. Came a rain, the cupboard fell all to pieces. It was *glued;* it went to pieces.

The night they shivareed us, they sneaked down the hill behind the shack. We were sitting there wondering when they would come. When anyone was married, they were shivareed, a sort of initiation into married bliss. They were very quiet until they got on top of that little knoll. All of a sudden, my land, I think every one of them had a .22 or a shotgun of some kind. They shot the stovepipe so full of holes the stove smoked. We couldn't even make coffee. Oh, they were wicked! We couldn't have a fire until the next day when Selah went to town and got another stovepipe.

I had sandwiches, and I think I'd baked some cookies. Look how little it cost, and the fun they had! The price of a new stovepipe . . . and that was probably a quarter.

The neighbors considered Marie to be a city girl whose marriage wouldn't last six months, but she quickly proved them wrong by working hard on the ranch.

We'd lived on a farm part of my life. Mother never did any outside work, but I started right in. I didn't learn to milk right away, but I stacked hay that first summer. You mowed the hay, then you had to rake it into long windrows. You went along with a pitchfork and put it in cocks. When you came with the hayrack and team, you loaded those cocks onto the hayrack, hauled it to the house, pitched it off the hayrack, and started a haystack. You've got to keep your hay out, so you don't get it all in the center, or it'd come to a peak too soon. A good many steps, and it didn't take me long to learn to build a real good stack of hay.

All horse-drawn equipment. We got a tractor about two years before we came up here [to Fairfield in 1937].

[I drove] old Nick and Ned. I've driven four horses to plow, driven a binder, I've shocked grain.

We cut the grain with the binder, then we'd go along and pick up all those bundles, put them in shocks. Come along with the wagon, throw them onto the hayrack. A lot of times they would put the bundles in a big stack, maybe out in the field or near a building. They call that stack threshing. It didn't take near as many men. As a rule, each man would have so many bundle racks, and they'd load it from the shocks right in the field. They'd load the wagons and haul it in to the threshing machine. A lot of steps compared to the combine they have now, one operation.

We had just the one room, so the first summer, in order to feed the threshers, we had to take down our bed and set it outside. We put a couple of little tables together [inside the house].

My mother came out from town to help me. Oh, such a little bit of a cookstove! I don't know how . . . Mother made the pies and baked the bread. To get the bread baked, and then to get our meat in to roast—it was a very small oven. Mother said she never worked so hard in her life.

The threshers brought their bedrolls. That first year we didn't have them very long, a couple of days. You had them for breakfast, dinner, and supper. Three meals, twenty men. They got very plain food: meat and pota-toes, bread and butter, and pie. Seems like we always made pie. Mother made the pies [the first year], but I soon learned. We had plenty of lard. I learned a lot the first few years we were married.

Down in the Winnett country, neighbors would go from one farm to the next [at threshing time]. It was an exchange of help. The women went and helped each other, too.

Many times it rained [at threshing]. Sometimes some of them stayed, but the majority of them went home. It depended upon the amount of rain. [If they stayed,] you just baked more bread and peeled more potatoes. If they had meat and potatoes, bread and gravy, they were satisfied. They didn't expect the variety people enjoy nowadays. They just didn't.

Marie took sewing in high school and had plans to be a home ec teacher, domestic science they called it. After getting married, she had to apply her skills at home.

My first baby's clothes were made out of my high school graduation dress. White voile. It was a full, pleated skirt with long sleeves. I used it to make Don's baby clothes, his dresses. We dressed babies differently than they do today. I used white flour sacks to make slips for the baby dresses. I bought outing flannel by the yard, [cut] and hemmed it to make diapers.

I bought my first sewing machine a short time after we were married. Bought it for ten dollars secondhand, and it took us a year to pay for it, a dollar at a time. I still have it. I piece quilts on it now. I've tried to use an electric machine, but I can't control the speed. I've tried, but I'll take the old treadle machine.

I made a lot of coats. My daughter didn't have a boughten coat until she was a freshman in high school. I made the boys' shorts out of flour sacks. Everything— flour, sugar, salt—came in cloth. I made handkerchiefs out of salt sacks; I could get that print out. Why, they made good handkerchiefs! Pure white, hemmed, 100 percent cotton. And they were ironed, too. Everything was ironed.

I've made pillowcases out of flour sacks. I've embroidered dozens of pairs. We never destroyed a sack. We used every one of them. A little later, the chicken feed was coming out in print [sacks]. Three sacks of chicken feed—all the same pattern—I made housedresses. And aprons. I didn't feel dressed if I didn't have an apron on.

You didn't change your dress every day; you wore an apron to protect it because you saved on washing. Now they can throw them in the machine, there's nothing to it. Let them wash on a board a while, they'll be more saving of their clothes.

I'll have to tell you a story. We didn't buy baby chicks, we set old hens. There was always an old settin' hen. You'd lock them up for so many days, and that was supposed to break them [of setting]. Well, I had two or three old hens. When they're setting, they're not laying. I'd shut them up a time or two, and they'd go right back to setting. I thought, "I'll fix them." So what did I do? I took three settin' hens off the nest, and I doused them in the water tank. I held them down as long as I dared, got 'em soaking wet, and turned them loose.

When my husband came in at noon for dinner, I said, "I sure fixed those old settin' hens this morning. I dumped them all in the water tank."

He slammed his fist down on the table. "That's the reason my team wouldn't drink that water!"

He was pretty perturbed at me for doing such, but I had no idea it would affect the horses. We had to dip all the water out of the tank and run fresh water in there.

I thought I'd give them a shock treatment. And it worked, it worked. But I got bawled out.

In the summer of 1918, before marrying Selah, Marie was staying at a friend's house and went to summer school in Lewistown. One night about midnight, the fire alarm woke them. The German textbooks had been taken out on the high school lawn and burned. A few days later, the high school was burned. They discovered several cans of gasoline in the building, so they knew it was definitely arson. Tension was high in Lewistown.

Many believed that the burning of the high school building was the work of a pro-German faction in retaliation for the book burning. Suspicion fell on the school's principal, a man of German background. He was arrested, tried, and acquitted. Those responsible for the school's destruction were never identified. The enmity that existed in the community was played out among the children at Marie's Pilgrim School as well.

One day a member of the school board visited school. He asked me if I was having trouble with any of the children, from one German family in particular. There were three children [from that family] coming to school. I said that a few days earlier, children were teasing one child, Otto.

"Who are you for, the Kaiser or the United States?"

He said, "For the Kaiser."

I was glad I was out there on the school ground, because I think there would have been a fight. I talked to them, and there was nothing serious to come of it. But I noticed a change in the attitude of Otto's parents toward me.

After I was married, we were living neighbors to these folks. They never came to our place. I could meet them on the street in town, and they ignored me. They didn't speak to me, but they'd speak to my husband.

Well, one Saturday when we were in Winnett, I met this family. They spoke and shook hands with me and were so pleasant. I couldn't understand it. And bless you, on Sunday they came over, Sunday afternoon about two o'clock. [They were] as friendly as could be. We visited right along, and when the men went out to do a few chores, I proceeded to get some supper. After they left, I said, "This is the biggest conundrum for me."

He told my husband, "I always felt your wife reported me as pro-German when she was teaching. I was up to Lewistown this last week—I rent some of the county attorney's land—and I said to him, 'The war's over, everything's settled, I wish you'd tell me who reported me as pro-German. I've always blamed the little school-teacher.'" The county attorney told him who it was. . . .

He never did apologize to me or mention it to me, but he had told my husband. We were neighbors, why not live as neighbors? From that time on, I thought nothing of it. We got along fine.

Politics in Lewistown, Montana, at the time was more important than one might think, and Marie's family took a particular interest.

My dad was a staunch Democrat. He always read *The Commoner,* a weekly paper published by William Jennings Bryan and his brother, Charles. That was really my dad's Bible.

William Jennings Bryan came to Lewistown in 1908 when he was running for the presidency. He spoke to the schoolchildren, and I've always remembered that he told us whenever a youngster said anything to him about dropping out of school, he said, "I give them a dull axe and send them out to the woodpile. After they've worked a while, I give them a good sharp axe and send them out. 'Can you see any difference?'" "Oh yes." "That's the difference in an education and no education. It's the same as a dull axe and a sharp axe." I've always remembered that.

He shook hands with all of us. I felt proud because my dad was a Democrat and a follower of William Jennings Bryan. He ran three times and was never elected. He was a brilliant man, a statesman. They called him "the silver-tongued orator."

The auditorium where he was to speak was completely filled, and there was such a big crowd outside, he said, "I'll speak to these in the auditorium first, then I'll speak to those outside. But I'll need some kind of a platform."

While he was speaking to those in the auditorium, the crowd waited outside, and they pulled up a manure spreader for his platform. When he came out to speak—William Jennings Bryan could always meet the occasion—he climbed up on the manure spreader, and he said, "This is the first time I've ever spoken from a Republican platform."

When Marie looked back, she marveled at the number of tasks she accomplished in a day's time.

When I think back, I wonder, how did I do all that? I'd get up in the morning; I'd make the bed before I left the bedroom. After breakfast I'd hurry and get the dishes washed while Selah was getting the team ready. We were married three years before we had any children, but after we had the children, I took them along with me.

My husband liked to go out and do the chores first, so it might be 7, 7:30 before we got breakfast. In the first years, when we had horses, he'd have them in and fed and harnessed, and after breakfast he'd be ready to go to the field.

Then I'd have washing or ironing to do, always sewing in between. I made all the kids' clothes. I churned, I baked bread. I milked my share of the cows, and [in later years] while I was getting breakfast, I'd have a batch of cookies in the oven so the kids'd have [them] in their lunch. I packed three lunches every morning. Summertime, there was garden work. As soon as I got the dishes done, I'd go to the garden.

In those days we had three substantial meals a day, breakfast, dinner, and supper. Many a morning I've had fresh fried potatoes, ham, milk gravy, baking powder biscuits. If you were out of bread, you had pancakes or baking powder biscuits or corn bread.

The youngsters were always so hungry when they came from school. My land, those boys would come home and eat a loaf of bread before they went out to do chores. Then they'd eat another loaf.

In the summertime, I tried to cook enough potatoes at noon so I wouldn't have to have the fire too long at night. On wash days, I always made a bread pudding or a rice pudding that I could have in the oven while I was using the top [of the stove]. It didn't make any difference how hot it was, you had to heat the [wash] water. You had to have the fire going on the days you ironed, too.

We bathed in the washtub, and we had no privacy. That's right, we just ignored it. We didn't wash our hair and bathe every day as they do now. Down at Winnett, water was such a premium that I bathed all the children in the same water. Then I took the bathwater and scrubbed the floor. You haul water in a barrel a quarter of a mile, you're going to be saving. The water that I rinsed the dishes in was the seed for the next batch of dishes. It was hard for me not to save water after I came up here [Fairfield]. I still can't waste anything, food, clothes. Waste not, want not.

The days I washed, we'd usually have to get another barrel that night. We had the barrel on an old stone boat. A stone boat is two pieces of wood, boards nailed across it. You set your barrel on the boards. They had a chain that the tugs were fastened to. You could haul a [water barrel] with one or two horses.

In the wintertime [when] you'd bring a barrel of water, you'd have to have a second barrel in the house. [As] you took a bucket and transferred water from one barrel to the next, there was dripping all along. It would freeze, and in no time you had a skating rink in the house!

In freezing weather, we had to put a tub over the top of the barrel [outside the house], a tub over the barrel in the house, and a tub over the top of the barrel on the stone boat. But in summer can you imagine how warm that water in the barrel got?

We had water right there at the house, near the barn, but it wasn't fit for drinking. It had so much alkali in it and so much iron. The longer you cooked potatoes, the harder they got. But the cattle and horses liked it; it was good stock water. We dug a well a quarter of a mile from the house. It was hard water, but it was good drinking water, and you could break it with soap.

How different wash day was! Get out the old boiler, put it on the stove, fill it with water—probably carry the water in from outside—heat the water, get the two washtubs on a bench with a washboard. Take the hot water out of the boiler, put it in the tubs, and rub those clothes with soap. And they had to be boiled, so they were put back in the boiler and boiled, then taken out with a stick and put into one of the tubs, go through two rinse waters and wrung. Clothes were wrung out by hand. Everything: blankets, sheets, overalls, everything! Your wrists would get so tired.

You had to take 'em out and hang 'em on the line, then bring 'em in and sprinkle 'em. Tablecloths, shirts, everything was starched and ironed. How did I iron? Heat your irons on the coal stove, have a pan over the top to keep the heat in it. I had four irons; I had to rotate in order to have a hot iron. If it got too hot, you'd scorch, and things scorched easily. Scorch is so hard to remove. You had to be careful, too, when you were using coal and wood not to get dirt on the iron. You had beeswax and paper at the end of the ironing board. Before you started to iron, you cleaned the iron good with the paper. The beeswax was used to make it glide smoothly.

My ironing board is makeshift; I've had it ever since I was married, and it's the only one I use. Put one end of the [ironing] table across the back of the chair, the other across the back of this chair. My son bought me one with legs. Heaven's sakes! I didn't like it, the thing wobbled. I gave it to my daughter. Look here, it needs a new cover. First time I have a sheet wear out, I'll have a new cover.

There was an order for hanging clothes. The sheets and pillowcases were washed and boiled first and hung out. Then there'd be the towels and dishtowels, tablecloths and underwear, socks, workshirts, overalls last.

There were times when you couldn't put clothes on the line. The snow'd be drifted up so it was near the line. Yes, that high. The snow would drift in there; it would be within a foot of the lines. We had to put the clothes on racks sometimes. They took a long time to dry because we couldn't wring them dry as a machine spins them now. Many a time I've put clothes on the line and they'd freeze so solid they'd tear easily, 'specially sheets. You'd bring them in, they're still stiff, but it doesn't take as long to dry them after they've been frozen.

We'd been married a few years before I learned to milk a cow. We had to milk more cows, have a little cream to sell. A five-gallon can of cream would bring us a dollar and a half, and that bought our groceries. Every now and then it could buy a pair of overalls for Selah, too. Eighty-nine cents for a pair of bib overalls.

I milked all the time, up until we sold the cows, about 1960. It's a seven-day-a-week job, summer, winter, oh dear! You forced yourself out [in the winter]. I always had on a pair of bib overalls, heavy socks and heavy overshoes, cap pulled down over my ears, a scarf pulled up over my nose.

When the boys were in service [World War II], we bought a milking machine. I was having lots of trouble with my hands; my hands were going to sleep. We doubled the number of milk cows and began selling whole milk rather than cream. I don't know as [a milking machine] does a better job, but they do as good a job, I'm sure. When we were milking, we had to take and empty the milking machines into a tank. Then the tank had to be emptied, the milk put into ten-gallon cans in the milk house. The cans were immersed in a tank of cold water, cool it as quickly as possible.

We ate so much cream . . . string beans, peas had to be creamed. There was cream on breakfast food, cream in our cottage cheese. Cream in the coffee. We should have been fat, but we burned up our calories. I weighed ninety-seven pounds for years and years. I was on the go all the time.

Very few people had dining rooms. Kitchens were big; everyone ate in the kitchen. The kitchen table was used for everything. *Everything!* Butcher—we cut up meat [on the table]. Patterns were laid out on the kitchen table. So many times, about the time you got your pattern laid out, it'd be time to get another meal. Fold it up and put it away.

If you had a room, a table, you could walk out and leave it. Leave it! That would be . . . I never had that.

We took milk down to the root cellar. And it wasn't really all that cool . . . I would say fifty degrees. The root cellar made lots of work. It wasn't just next door to the house . . . maybe half a block. If you wanted to do some cooking in the morning, you brought the milk down [to the house], then you had to take it back to the root cellar before noon, otherwise it would sour. At noon, if you wanted milk or cream or butter—oh, the trips back and forth to that root cellar.

Once a week I'd bake at least eight loaves of bread, and I'd bake baking powder biscuits in between. We used to buy yeast foam in a wooden box, dry squares, individually wrapped.

In the early days, you couldn't bake bread without potato water. The night before, you'd take your potato water, put a cake of yeast in it, and let it dissolve. Before you went to bed, you'd make a batter, just a small amount of flour, not really stiff. A good deal like cake batter. By morning that would have raised. In the wintertime, I left [dough overnight] on the back of the heater stove in the front room. It was an all-day job to make bread.

A lot of us made our own breakfast food. We'd take wheat, wash it good, put it in a double boiler, banked the fire on the heating stove in the front room. It slow-cooked all night, and by morning it was as tender as could be. You'd put some good rich cream on that wheat. I never used sugar, but Selah and the kids did. Whole wheat cereal, good and hot.

I've sold many a five-gallon can of cream for a dollar and a half. How many people would wash a separator seven days a week for a dollar and a half? There isn't a job more miserable than washing an old cream separator. Oh dear, I think I dreaded that the worst of anything on the farm. To wash that old cream separator!

I knew if I didn't do it in the morning . . . the only way to do it was to get it over with in the morning. The longer you put it off, the worse it was. How many steel discs were there? Fifty, seventy-five, something like that. I hung them on the back of the separator after they were washed. Some people hung them on the clothesline, but they'd get so full of dust you'd have to wash them again when you put the separator together at night.

It was quite a chore to run [the separator] by hand. The hardest part was getting it up to speed before you turned the milk in. That took muscle, strength, and it had to be up there before it would work. You could tell when you had it up to the right speed.

We used to buy a ton of coal for the heater stove in the front room, and that would last us all winter. We'd use it only in the real cold weather and at night to bank. Other than that, we used wood. Down in the Winnett country, you could go down to the creek and get plenty of wood. Up here at Fairfield there was very little available wood. We used to buy railroad ties. Selah would go and get a load—those ties made good [fuel] but oh, they were dirty.

I've helped saw wood time and time again. I never would let Selah work alone with that buzz saw. I was always out there; it's a very dangerous job.

The two older children, Don and Gene, were born at the home of a midwife in Winnett. The other two, Earl and Alta Mae, were born at home. Those days, you couldn't raise your head; we stayed in bed for ten days. I never went to the doctor [during pregnancy]. I knew I was pregnant. I didn't need him to tell me. None of the women ever went to him before [delivery]. He'd see me on the street. . . . "I'll be called to Converses one of these days." That's all there was to it! For Alta Mae and Earl, it was just a friend's mother who came and took care of me and the baby.

I thought [the births] were hard enough, but I never had any complications. Everything went as it was supposed to, and I got along fine. Alta Mae was born in July, and oh, it was hot. The water stood in the barrel; I couldn't even have a cold drink of water. And you couldn't have a cup of coffee without building a fire!

The babies slept with us a lot [in very cold weather]. Now they wouldn't think of doing it. They say it isn't good for the child. Didn't hurt mine to sleep with us. I loved to cuddle down to them.

I never took my children to the doctor. I would say they were very healthy. Turpentine was our antiseptic. They cut their fingers, we had the turpentine. Wrap it, use a cloth. [For colds,] just grease 'em with goose grease. Grease their backs, the bottoms of their feet, grease their chests. Every one of my children had what they called the croup. And that used to scare me. I always kept some alum on hand. Alum, mixed with a little bit of sugar, would cut the phlegm in their throats.

In the fall, it seemed like the first whiff of cool air, they'd come in with the croup. I'd have to keep them in the house, give them alum and sugar, and grease 'em up good. And I've made onion syrup for colds. You boil those onions, boil them and boil them and boil them and add a little sugar. You let it boil down until the syrup is a brown color.

It seemed like when we were raising our family there was always so much to do outside, but Selah was real good. If he came in and dinner wasn't quite ready, he'd take the baby and hold it until I finished up the meal. While he never did any of the washing, or I can't say that he ever changed their diapers, he was good about taking them with him when he went someplace, if he could. If he was going to run in to town for a little bit, he'd take them.

I've always thought that farm and ranch families that didn't have at least a few children must have found the workload heavy. There was always a barn to clean or pigs to feed, calves to feed, hay and straw to haul in. Bed the barn down, bed the sheds down, there was always work outside.

A farm's a wonderful place to bring up a family. Children learn how to work, and it's a good place to learn the facts of life in a natural way. I think they keep out of mischief. Of course, farm life has been modernized, but there're still things to do.

You know the cleanest animal? A pig! They are. They have one spot in their pen for their bathroom. How many other animals have that? Oh, little pigs, they're the cutest of all animals. I like pigs.

One morning Selah said, "We've got to take pigs from this old sow." He had the old sow in a pen where he figured she'd be all right. He was on the other side of the fence, and I said, "You can hand them to me."

I was in the pen, catching the pigs. First thing you know, the old sow had gotten out. I had two pigs in my hands, and this old sow was coming right toward me. He was hollering, "Drop those pigs, Marie! Drop those pigs!"

I knew I was going to make it over the fence, and he was sure I wouldn't. He had a hammer in his hand; he threw it at that old sow, hit her in this vital spot, right in the center of the head, and she dropped instantly. Deader than dead. She had raised ten pigs, and she was a rail, not fit for meat or anything else. She was hauled down to the coulee for the coyotes. They cleaned her up in no time.

Maybe I was a little foolish, but I had those pigs and I wasn't going to let loose of them. I got the pigs over the fence!

I always raised a big garden [on the Fairfield ranch]. We got our peas right from the field. The field peas that we raised were the seed to be raised by canneries as canning peas. I canned ninety quarts of peas the first summer we were up there. We hadn't had vegetables for so many years. We ate ninety quarts of peas that first year.

Did you ever hear of shelling peas with a washing machine? Oh, that is neat! My neighbor and I canned fifty-four quarts of peas—fifty-four—in one day. Picked, shelled, and canned.

We had an oil-burning stove and a boiler out in the milk house. We'd take and put a bucket of peas in a flour sack and put them in the boiling water for two to three minutes, take 'em out, and dip 'em in a tub of cold water. I'd take the agitator out [of the washing machine], dump the peas in there, put a sheet over my head and over the machine, then scoop the peas up and put them through the wringer. The pods go through and the peas fall back into the machine. I think of those fifty-four quarts we didn't have a quart of squashed peas.

It works so slick! The minute those pods hit the wringer, they pop! You pack them into jars, put in a teaspoon of salt and water. My boiler would hold sixteen quarts. We'd bring the water two inches over the top of the jars, boil them for three hours. I lost very few peas, very few.

That was our Sunday night lunch. When the boys were home, they usually had another boy or two with them. I'd open two quarts of those peas and cream them and then I'd make toast. Creamed peas over toast was our Sunday night lunch. We gradually got our fill so they didn't taste near as good as they had at first.

I never canned carrots; we could keep them down in our basement. Put them down there, put sand over them and they kept real well. And rutabagas, lovely potatoes and onions, and oh, so many string beans. And we had our meat and our eggs. Our milk checks bought our groceries, absolutely. Coffee was only twenty-five cents a pound.

The schoolhouse was the center of entertainment. Families would go there, take a cake, a few sandwiches, pay the fiddler twenty-five cents, and have a whole evening's entertainment.

I have a deaf ear for music; still, it didn't keep me from dancing. I love to dance. "It's a Long Way to Tipperary" was one song [the fiddler played]. And "I'm

Forever Blowing Bubbles," "When the Boys Come Marching Home." We did the hippity-hop, the two-step, lots of schottisches and quadrilles, square dances and waltzes, lots of waltzes. The waltzes were just beautiful. The music of today—I don't call it music—dum, dum, dum.

We never thought of going home before two or three o'clock in the morning. Most of the time we fell into bed, but we'd have to get up and milk the cows. Those cows weren't on as strict a schedule as a dairy, so if we were an hour or so late, it was no killing matter. We'd get up and do the chores, maybe have a bit of breakfast, then fall back into bed.

In the wintertime, you'd get down to the school-house, and you'd have to drain the radiator in the old Model T and bring the water in. Then when you got ready to go home, take that water back out, fill the radiator, crank the old Model T, and away you'd go. Ours didn't have a top. Oh, that old hard wind would be so cold. Selah's dad sent us a fur robe, a bear robe. That was a lifesaver! When we got a sedan with a top, we thought we were somebody. . . .

We had a pretty good crop the first year we were married, and not too bad the second. In 1928 we had what we considered a wonderful crop. I don't remember how many bushels [to the acre] we had, but we paid up all our expenses in the fall.

In 1929 we had just half the yield we'd had in 1928. We'd put in a crop every spring, but for nine straight years, from '28 on, we didn't even get our seed back. We took out government loans. The government gave us enough money to buy seed to plant the next year. . . .

The grain might get up so we could cut it and use it for hay. And then we put up Russian thistles. Well, there again, they must be cut. Put them up a good deal the same as you would hay. You went out and mowed them. The main thing was to cut them before they were prickly. The cows ate them; they made good feed if you didn't have anything else. Selah always thought it improved the flavor to put in a little salt as he stacked it.

And then in the '30s we had the grasshoppers. They came in swarms; they would darken the sky. They'd get in the house in spite of you; they'd come in on your back. They ate everything. Everything! They actually cleaned out my houseplants. They ate all my curtains. They did! They stripped my curtains, plain cotton material.

In 1936 the government instigated the resettlement program. They would buy our land and resettle us. They had different projects; we could take our choice. We looked at two or three places; one was in the Bitterroot [Valley] not far from Hamilton. We came up here [to Fairfield] and looked this over and decided this was where we wanted to come.

We wanted to go where there was plenty of water and no wind. Well, you can't have everything. We had plenty of water, but there's plenty of wind. But the dirt didn't blow like it did in a three hundred-acre sand blizzard down there in Winnett. That was open prairie, and of course there are a lot of trees around here. We planted all those trees. They were furnished by the government, but we had to plant them.

My husband came up in July of '37 and brought one load, the horses and what machinery we had. Our house wasn't done at that time, so the youngsters and I stayed down to Winnett, and on the thirteenth of October, Mr. Bowers brought our household goods, and my folks brought the youngsters and me in their car. So you see, we didn't have a crop that year. Selah had worked with the furnished threshing crew. We had brought only two milk cows with us. The first thing, one cow went out that fall and bloated on some alfalfa. We lost her, but the government had issued us an operating loan and we bought a few more cows. We lived on cream checks that winter, the winter of '37–'38. It was an open winter [little snowfall].

When we came here on the thirteenth of October, they hadn't even started the house on our place. We were sharing another resettlement house with a family a mile out of town, another resettlement family whose house wasn't done. The last day of December in '37, we moved into our new house. Selah moved our stuff on the hayrack, and he was in his shirtsleeves. It was that nice a day.

There were four [resettlement house] designs. We had three bedrooms, living room, dining room, and kitchen. The dining and living room had a partition, and the rooms were small. One day I got busy and tore out that partition. I thought for a while I was going to lose my happy home. My husband—I did it one day when he was gone—said, "We haven't paid for this place; you're going to get into trouble."

The farm manager and home supervisor called one day. Selah and the farm manager were in the kitchen talking; the home supervisor and I were in the living room. She noticed what had been done. "Oh," she said, "this is so much nicer," and she called the farm manager in to see it. I told her I'd done it. She thought it was a good idea. My taking out the partition, it was a nice-sized room. Putting the heating stove in the corner in the living room, you made it one big room. It was much easier to heat.

I didn't get into any trouble. I know there was more than one that followed suit.

We owed the government ten thousand dollars [for] an operating loan to buy machinery, cows, or horses, whatever we needed, plus the price of the land. I thought, "We never in this world will be able to pay that off." But we did! Where we made our mistake—hindsight is better than foresight—we could have taken forty years to pay for that place at 3 percent. But we had been in debt all of our married life, and our only goal was to be free of debt. We had an especially good clover seed crop one year, and we paid practically all of it off. We had paid off the operating loan. There were some who took at least thirty-five years [to pay off their loans]. They made that small payment each year and went out and bought more land. To start with, we had only the eighty acres, but soon they wanted so much diversification: have a small patch of peas, a small patch of sugar beets, a small patch of oats, some hay ground and pasture. Eighty acres doesn't give you [much]. Some of the resettlers moved; some of them they shifted around. In a few years, we were given another forty acres, 120 acres altogether. And that's all we ever had. Oh, we had to buy it; the forty acres was extra.

Thirty-five families came from Winnett. There were several of them who became discouraged, and as soon as they got a few dollars ahead, they left. They hadn't paid for their places, but whoever moved onto that place assumed the balance of the land payments.

[With] so much government regulation, [people] felt their freedom was taken away from them. We never felt that, although they had a mortgage on everything, on our stock and on the land, but any other loaning agency would have done the same. We did have to make out a family farm plan, and a family budget once a year. Any good business does that.

They filled out the expenses for the coming year and your income for the coming year. They also reported what you actually did produce that year, what your actual income was. It's nothing more than good business. But oh, so many of them, they had never done anything like that. They didn't know the first principle of bookkeeping, and they resented it. The first couple of years, all of our checks were countersigned. As soon as the government understood that you really were sincere and wanted to make a go of it, they took off that restriction.

The main objection: They didn't want to be told what to do.

The majority of [the people who had owned the resettled land] were in the same fix we were in. They had to sell half of their farm—most were 320 [acres]—in order to pay the back taxes and keep the other half. In one way, they weren't any better off than we were, financially. If the government hadn't bought some of their land, the county would have taken it over for [back] taxes.

There was a resentment in the community to the resettlers. Some of them came right out and said the government was giving us all this. The government didn't give us anything except *opportunity*.

One woman made the remark that she couldn't understand the government sending the scum of the earth here. You see, there were so many people with bedbugs—brought them with them. A letter came from the office telling us how to get rid of the bedbugs. They sent every resettler one of those letters. It didn't bother us any, we didn't have bedbugs, and we realized they had to send to everybody. But oh, some of them, they were really mad about it. They didn't need the government to tell them how to get rid of bedbugs!

We hadn't been here too long when a neighbor lady called on me and invited me to her home to meet with the ladies of the church. Her living room was full of ladies; she introduced me to all of them. They were pleasant and all. This one lady sitting next to me began talking, asking all kinds of questions. While I felt she *knew* I was a resettler—I was an absolute stranger in the crowd—she wanted to make sure.

She finally said, "How many children do you have?"

I said, "Four. Three boys and a girl."

"Oh, you're not a resettler then, are you?"

The remark had been made that all the resettlers knew was to raise big families and dance! I assured her that even though we had only four children, we were still resettlers.

Maybe I should feel my age, but I don't. I have to look in the mirror to realize that I am as old as I am. I've been blessed with good health. I realize I can't do the work that I did, but I can work pretty good for a couple of hours and then I need a coffee break.

I've kept interested in people. I haven't read as much as I would like to have, but anything I do read is good material. I guess soap operas are all right, but I'd rather sit down and work a crossword puzzle or read a book. I like to crochet; I've made several afghans. I'm busy all the time. I don't sit down and twiddle my thumbs. In the evening, after I've read a while, oh, I'm tired, I might just sit for a little while. . . .

It takes me much longer to do anything. Goodness sakes, I used to get up and have a couple of pies in the oven before breakfast!

Marie Converse was interviewed at her home in Fairfield, Montana, in November 1987. She died there in 1990 at age ninety-two.

URMA DELONG TAYLOR

"... down in the root cellar. ...
They crocheted, and I played with frogs."

Urma DeLong Taylor was born in Solen, North Dakota, on December 22, 1911. Her parents and her mother's family, the Geers, were to become part of Montana's great homestead saga. When she spoke of those years, 1915 to 1919, it was sometimes with sadness, but also with nostalgia, pride, and triumph.

Urma was a kind and loving woman. And a born storyteller who spoke with a slight Irish brogue. Though she suffered from arthritis, she never complained. She was someone who knew responsibility; in fact, she had assumed it since her early childhood. By the time she was ten, she was baking and cooking for her family.

In 1915, when she was three and a half, Urma traveled with her parents, John and Elata DeLong, and her older sister, Hester, in a covered wagon, from their home in Mott, North

Dakota, to Colorado. The wagon was built and outfitted by John, a carpenter by trade.

It looked like all pictures of covered wagons, bows up over the top with canvas. It was waterproof, 'n' had that little puckerin' string that we'd peek out and watch the scenery as we'd gone past it. It was all cupboards on the inside. They were along the side, had doors on 'em so things wouldn't rattle out. Some was shelving, part was drawers. Ever'thing had to have a door on it. On the outside he built shelves to carry the barrels of water and feed for the horses.

In the cupboards there were cans of all descriptions [and] size, according to the food that was in 'em. You could put fifty pounds of flour in one of those cans. They nearly always bought sugar in twenty-fives.

Mother had an old-fashioned dutch oven. It had three little legs, a lid, and a handle to pick it up by. She made her biscuits in it, right over the campfire. And you never tasted better biscuits. There was a hotcake griddle, skillets, coffee pot 'n' such. She had a wire grill, and it had legs you could stick in the ground above the open fire, with a utensil on it.

Mother had lovely feather beds and homemade quilts. In them days, instead of a mattress, everybody had their feather beds. We all slept in that little space that was in the center between the cupboards. A wagon is not awfully wide. Every morning she spread the bedding out good, 'n' we played on that all day long.

You've seen pictures of covered wagons, how they had a bench along the side. You put water in wooden kegs on both sides. And then when you come up on a place where somebody had a well or a spring, then you'd replenish all of your water. We had a number of jugs and jars that we carried inside for ourselves. But if the barrels got too empty, you'd share that with the horses. You had to water your horses even if you had to go a little short.

On that trip, we did what many a person couldn't say they'd done—they're so fussy about water nowadays—we took a cup and reached into a foot track. It had rained pretty hard in this one area, and some cattle had crossed there, and where they stepped down kinda deep, it was nothin' at all to dip in and get a drink. Never give contamination a thought. In those days, water was water. Wet was wet.

Mother always sat up in the seat with Father as they drove along. When one of 'em's arms got tired, the other one could take over. She was ever' bit as good a horseperson as he was.

One time we crossed—I think Mother called it the Little Missouri River. It was in the spring, and it was pretty swollen. The horses had to swim some before they got to the edge. When they went to pull up out of there onto the bank, us girls rolled right down and hit the tailgate of the wagon. Mother thought, out we went to drown! It was just the noise of a heavy chain from the outside hittin' the back end. It held, but she just about had a heart attack.

You got your clothes washing done when you came to a stream. You was just mighty careful of water. I've not gotten over all of it, either. We'd all wash our hands out of the same pan. Us little children's hands wasn't as dirty as the daddy's was, so he'd be the last one that used that water.

People today, they don't know the hardships people used to have. There's too much waste goes on. That gets me. Throw away things. They get so far ahead in stuff they don't know what to do with it.

Whenever they could, the DeLongs lived off the land.

They would kill grouse, ducks, if they found some of those, and fish. Different kinds of little things like that. We stopped at stores to buy things. We ate a lot of dried fruit: apricots, prunes, peaches, apples. Mother had made jams and jellies; she'd canned a lot, of course. She had canned beef and chicken, but you couldn't carry along much.

Mother cooked ahead whatever she could so they didn't have to stop every mealtime. You never wasted even a hotcake. You put butter and sugar on it, stacked it up, and that would be lunch lots of times.

Us girls slept in until we was ready to get up. They'd be on the road by that time. We had hotcakes or something that we could snack on until Mother cooked the next meal.

She didn't try to cook if it was raining. She had to have food that we could get by on, like opening a can of sardines and such.

When the DeLongs finally reached their destination, a great disappointment awaited them. They had made that lengthy journey on the strength of an advertisement for the development of a new town.

They had advertised for carpenters to make a town. You had to have two thousand dollars cash or the equivalent of it. Father didn't have that much; I think it was five hundred dollars. He figured with that fine team and wagon and his tools he made up more than two thousand. They didn't want a bunch of poor people comin' in there. After we got to the town, they had decided to change their minds. They didn't make the town, so there's nothin' to do but turn around and go back.

Coming back, it was getting late enough, there was lots of gardens. If they was near enough to a ranch, they'd go and ask about buying some. Otherwise, if a garden was close to the edge of the road, you borrowed a few. The idea was, you took only enough to do 'til you come to the next garden. By not planning that trip back, we was running very short of money.

They headed north to Sheridan, Wyoming, where John worked as a carpenter. From Sheridan, they went to Broadus, Montana, where they joined the Geers, Elata's parents and siblings.

My father put in for a homestead out of Broadus, where my grandparents' ranch was. My mother's brothers and sisters, all of them, was living right in that same area. Father went to a land office and made out the papers for the homestead, come home, and Mother's brothers helped him get the logs out and make it. I have a picture of the house they built.

We wintered in it, and the next spring along come a man, and he said, "What are you folks doing here?" "Why," my father said, "this is my homestead. We built the house and wintered here."

"Well, I'm sorry," he said, "but you're on my land." And my father says, "All right, where did you put in for yours?" And I think they said it was some twenty or thirty miles away at another land office. So, to prove the thing, they go over to the land office, and they get the timing, because it was put down right to the minute when you signed the paper, and then they got the timing at the other one. *Three hours difference,* and it was *his* land. We had to pick up and leave, go someplace. There was no more land right around there. It was a fam'ly thing: We had our house to live in, but we all worked together, we all shared our food. Food and some clothes was all you thought of anyhow.

This one brother [of my mother's] had got him a place. He and his bride had been living with his folks. This went on lots of times, 'til you had children and they made a little more ruction. He didn't have a house yet, so what they done, they put [our house] on a couple of skids 'n' hauled it over to his land. He bought the cabin from [my folks]. He'd helped build it, too.

After the homestead, we went down eastward from Sheridan. Got a eighty-acre place there thirteen miles out of Arvada [Wyoming]. It would get so HOT in the summertime, and of course we'd go barefoot. It'd feel like it was burning your feet on the floor in the house. Right after breakfast, my mother and sister and I, we'd plan what we was goin' to have for lunch, and we'd hurry and fix it, and take it down in the root cellar. We'd spend the whole day there. They crocheted, and I played with frogs. I diapered them and everything. They reminded me of a little child. When I lay them down to put their diapers on, they just lay there and let me do it. I had more fun with my little frogs!

I never rode in a car once in the time we lived there near Arvada. Oh, if us kids didn't look forward to the day when it was time to go to town. I don't recall ever going to town in the wintertime. It'd always be so cold, but in the summertime, my mother drove the team, and we went in the wagon to town. Oh, boy, you'd get a few sticks of candy, little odds and ends like that. We sent to the catalog for things. Practically everything you got, you got outta catalogs. I never will forget, there in the post office in town, some new shoes for me. Oh, those leather shoes! You know what leather smells like; that was the best perfume I'd ever smelled. As we went along, ever' few minutes, I'd take 'em out, oh, put 'em on, look 'em over, then put 'em back in the box. That was my fun, all the way home. 'Course, you never wore 'em around home. You only wore 'em when you went somewhere. Set 'em on the shelf, I'd pert near wear 'em out takin' 'em down to smell 'em.

The things that would please a child then, they wouldn't even think of today.

In contrast to the hot summers at Arvada, Urma describes some of the consequences of a severe winter there.

It sounded like guns a-poppin' when the cottonwood trees were cracking from bein' frozen. There were big old chunks of ice settin' ever' which way [in the river]. They were so huge they looked like rooms.

When the ice went out in the spring, when the water started comin' down from above, you had no way of tellin' unless a horseback rider come along sayin', "Be careful, here it comes." The water come a-gushin' through there, it was an awful mess. It took a long time before the ice was all melted away.

Our neighbor, they'd always raised quite a lot of pigs. So their pigs would have a drink, they'd run a fence down in the river. They had a big cloudburst, miles and miles above. It looked like the ocean when it hit there. The poor old pigs, they were almost ready for butchering, so you know how fat they'd be under their jowls. When that thing hit, it hit with a bang. They tried to swim, but hogs aren't much for swimming. As they were trying to swim to shore, head to higher ground, they cut their own throats. Their hooves stabbed into their jowls as they were making the motion to swim. Some drowned right there in the pen in the river.

That hard winter, 1918 going into '19, ruined the Geer family's big cattle business. They died like flies. There was nothin' for them to eat. The old swamp hay they was bringin' in from North Dakota was all there was to be had, and they couldn't afford it. Cattle wasn't worth enough. They had bins of corn, so they saved a few, but it was nothing but a handful. It broke their hearts. They sold out to a neighbor, their land, their cattle, their equipment 'n' everything, and they pulled out. The boys went wherever they could to find work.

The grandparents took off and went out to . . . a ways from Seattle, in that general area. They wrote back and says, "Say, there's fruit picking and things to make a living at out here. You better, any of you that wants something to do, come."

My mother and her sister and us two girls went out there. My dad didn't come right then. He wanted to see whether we ended up a visit or what.

We got in right at raspberry picking time, then it went to cherry picking. Us kids would do whatever the grown-ups was doing. It felt so funny to be makin' some money! When it come fall, we went down to Vancouver, that one across from Portland. They had this big Del Monte packing plant where they canned every type of fruit, vegetable, anything in season, and they got on there.

In Vancouver we had tent houses. You see, the winters never got bad like here. They had a coal-oil-burning stove with a little coal-oil pot set over to the side that fed either two or three burners.

There was city water; you had a faucet outside where you could go and carry water in pails. Of course, you had your washtub because you had to wash clothes by hand. There were outside toilets everywhere. Other than the lovely modern homes that were already built, anywhere you lived, you always had to have your outside.

Mother showed me how I could boil spuds or fry 'em, usually boil. Then when they came home to lunch, nearly always it was hamburger. That or bacon, sump'n on that order to fix real quick.

In addition to cooking, Urma, who was eight and a half, was solely responsible during the day for watching over Hester, her older sister.

You see, my sister had epilepsy, and they couldn't depend on her for many things. She could do some items, but mainly I had to carry on, and I was younger. There were two or three years that she was in a home in Spokane, and I was on my own entirely.

When I was a kid, my folks used to say, "You do whatever you're supposed to do, all your chores. When you get all your work done, then you can play with the neighborhood children. But you give them to understand that there's no playin' goes on 'til your work is done."

My mother taught me to bake bread when I was ten or eleven years old. She'd stir up the starter the night before and set the alarm for the next morning to wake me. I was to jump up and make it from there, bake bread for supper. Fresh-made bread for supper.

The days she had off, she'd teach me this or that. The summer I was ten and a half, she took me out and said, "OK, now I'm going to show you how to dress chickens." We had no refrigeration whatsoever. You killed the chicken that day—I had an old gent do that for me—bleed it out good. Have hot water in your teakettle,

85

pour that over it so the feathers'll come off, then pick the feathers. Cut it open at the back end, reach in and get the entrails out. Cool it. You have to keep catching more cold water, cool the meat good and thorough for all those hours 'til it's suppertime. Then you fix it. You didn't try to hold anything for the next day.

One day I asked some girls, "How many of you can dress a chicken from the feathers on, cut it up, and have a meal on the table at night?" Well, they could none of them say it, of course.

Maybe that made me feel cocky, doin' something the rest of 'em didn't do. But with my mother working all the time. . . .

In the Arvada segment, Urma tells a story about Pete, a little orphaned chicken.

Down there out of Arvada was a place where the road went right through a man's barn lot. You had to open a gate, go through it, then open another. This one day there was a poor little chicken, and he couldn't keep up with Mama for the reason that he'd gotten into some horse hair, and it had wound around and made hobbles of his little feet. Mother went to the house to tell 'em about it. There was not a soul nowhere, at the barns or anywhere, so we took the little orphan home with us. We got that old hair off. We named him Pete, and he was a spoiled child. He lived right in the house with us; he's one of us. We didn't put him in a cage; we put him in a box for the night.

I never will forget this one time; we was doing things outside and had left him there in the house. To this good day, I do what my mother did: On my table here's salt 'n' sugar 'n' everything. Sugar bowl settin' there, quite a big one. He jumped up on the table, and the highest thing he found was the sugar bowl. When we come in, he was perched there on the edge. He wasn't even half-grown, just a teeny myguy yet, havin' to babysit himself. [Sadly] Oh, kid, such funny things. . . .

Urma Taylor was interviewed at my home in Pray, Montana, in May 1985 and again in November 1987. She died in 1999 at her home in Pray. She was eighty-seven years old.

WINIFRED CHOWNING JEFFERS

"The butchering process?
Oh dear, I didn't ever watch it!"

Winifred Chowning Jeffers was a tall woman, proper and well-educated. She demanded—and was used to getting—respect. She talked of the past while sitting among the furniture that had once belonged to her grandparents. Winifred's maternal grandfather was William Ennis, for whom the town of Ennis, Montana, is named, and she proudly told of the part he had played in settling the town.

My grandfather came here in 1863 from Omaha, Nebraska. He had been at Pike's Peak because gold was discovered there. When the gold played out, he figured he ought to move someplace where he could use all his equipment. He made a trip to Alder Gulch, because gold had been discovered near Virginia City [Montana]. Originally, he had a small store and a pasture where he kept some freighting animals. When he first came, he built a log cabin. Later, he built a large house, which burned down in 1917.

Everybody came into Virginia City in those days with teams. They came because of the gold rush on the Alder Gulch. They needed supplies, and that's why he had outfitted in Omaha with all the necessary things. He had drovers to help him. When he came over the hill from Virginia City, there was no road; he had to pick his way over here. When he saw the lovely grass and hay that was here, he said, "We're going to stop right here. We're not going to look any farther." Later, he took up a homestead. It had never been surveyed up 'til the time he got here.

He had a lot of stock: oxen, mules, and horses for his freighting business. Of course, they needed a lot of feed. He took up what they called squatter's rights on this land out here. He took it up the same day my grandmother gave birth to my mother, Jenny Winifred Ennis, back in Iowa, August 13, 1863.

My father came out here as a young man. His people, the Chowning family, had lived in Kentucky, moved to Indiana, and then to Missouri, but I don't know the dates. He had gone to the University of Missouri and was almost ready to graduate, but he became sick, left school, and came west for his health. He got a job in Helena working for the Northern Pacific Railroad that was outside work. He came here to evaluate and locate the Northern Pacific sections that had been given to them by the government, to encourage the Northern Pacific to build out into the rural areas.

Winifred was born on August 7, 1895, in Ennis in her grandmother's house, which has since burned down. She went to school in Jeffers, across the Madison River.

My mother didn't let me go until I was seven, because she was so afraid of that river. When she was a little girl, there was just a wooden bridge, and sometimes the gorge took it out. The water'd be a lot deeper wherever the gorge was. My grandmother used to walk down there and watch to make sure she came across safely when the gorge was running. Mother never got over the fear of that water.

We always carried lunch, usually sandwiches and perhaps an apple. I don't think it was even thought of, to have a warm lunch.

The walk to the one-room schoolhouse at Jeffers was a mile and a half. The school went to the eighth grade.

After I'd gone to school one year at Jeffers, there were three or four other families that decided to band together and try to get a school district on our side of the river.

First, they had to petition to get a school district, and after they got that, they had to tax themselves to get money enough to build a schoolhouse. At first, they just partitioned off a part of the dance hall for their school.

All my life I've lived here except when I was away to boarding school. We had no high school here, and my people were very anxious for me to continue right on as soon as I was out of the eighth grade. I went to All Saints School in Sioux Falls, South Dakota, run by the Episcopal Church. I'm very proud to say that I was elected proctor at the end of my first year, and I served as proctor for the rest of the years that I was there. When I graduated, I was given a gold medal.

Although Winifred had many happy recollections of her time spent at All Saints School, she spoke more often of her childhood memories of her Grandmother Ennis.

The first house my grandmother lived in was one that Grandpa built when he came over the hill from Virginia City looking for land for his horses and oxen. They just cut some logs—native trees—and threw up some kind of shelter.

When Grandma came, that's what she moved into. Then Grandpa bought a log house in Virginia City, took it apart, and brought it here. They set it up first at the end of Main Street; later they moved it. In 1882 they had a new house built. They had to have the lumber sawed; it took quite a while to get all the things together to make it. This furniture, that was part of her house. It was part of a set, the sofa and the four chairs that go with it. When their house burned [in 1917], that furniture was saved. Grandma willed it to my mother, and I've willed it to the museum in Bozeman [Museum of the Rockies].

My grandmother had a beautiful home after she got out of that log house. She was great for trying to fix things up a little bit fussy every once in a while.

I can recall her kitchen. She had a large stove and a real large reservoir on the side of the stove. My grandmother was a very ingenious woman. She had a pipe that went from the reservoir across the ceiling and down the other side of the house, down the side wall. It was connected to the pump and the well that was under the house. She could turn a faucet on the pump and fill the reservoir by pumping.

She had a makeshift bathroom off the kitchen. A tinsmith from Virginia City had made a large tub for the place. She had pipes that ran from the hot water tank. Hot water would run into the bathtub, but you had to carry the cold water in a bucket. It was so much different from what most people had, you know. That was her own ingenious plan.

I loved to be with my grandmother. It seemed like she was always doing something. She talked to me a great deal. I went to help her hunt turkey hens' nests. They were domestic, but they were pretty wild. They hid out, you know. Lots of times I helped her if she wanted to fix up some fence. I'd go with her; she had a special bucket, a brass bucket, that she carried her tools in and the staples to fix the fences up.

She enjoyed working out of doors. I think it was pretty hard on her to have been confined to the house later. She fell and had a broken hip.

It was always a great treat to be with my grandmother. I don't remember my grandfather. He died when I was about two.

Winifred's grandfather had a general store. When he died, her mother inherited the store and ran it with the help of her husband.

It was up to her to make a success of it. People brought butter into the store to trade for groceries. My father never turned it down; he always took it. It didn't make any difference who made it. We knew one woman who always made such nice butter. We always wanted to get her butter.

Butter for food. They got credit for the butter, and then they bought other groceries. Some people ran a tab, some didn't pay at all, and some were very prompt.

Sometimes butter had to be thrown out because it hadn't been worked enough or something like that. We had a cellar at the store that we kept it in. After a while, the butter didn't smell too good. It gets a little sour. Maybe a quarter of it had to be thrown out.

I'll say this about my mother and father. There was never a disagreement in my hearing. Children should be taught to respect their parents when they're little. My mother told me I couldn't do something one time when I was little, so I went to talk to my father. I thought maybe he'd let me do it. I was a schemer when I planned to do that. He said, "What does your mother say?" I said,

"She said 'no.'" "Then that's the way it is," he said. I've often thought about that. My respect for him increased, let me tell you.

When Winifred's mother assumed responsibility for the general store, a hired girl was employed to look after the house.

She had a hired girl in the house here. Sometimes it was a local girl. At one time she had a girl and her brother from the Ruby Valley. They were companions, and they weren't too lonesome. Naturally they ate with the family! You weren't merely a hired girl; you were a friend. I don't know how many years they were here, but they always remained fast friends with my people.

The many social activities in the town enlivened Winifred's childhood and teen years.

You went with your friends to dances, Fourth of July celebrations, and things like that. You were invited to homes, you played games.

Visiting was kind of a difficult proposition. You always had to go with a team of horses because the homesteads were two or three miles apart. When anybody came, you expected them to stay all day because it was quite a trip to get here. When my mother went to visit someone, she'd be gone all day. I'd usually stay with my grandmother.

Almost always they had a Fourth of July celebration. We looked forward to that. They used this Main Street [where Winifred's home is located] for a racetrack, and the horses bucked up and down. I've seen them mark off the distance on the street. They had saddle-and-go races. I don't remember that they had fireworks. They were given more to having a dance at night. The dance hall is where we had our first school, a lodge hall upstairs and a dance hall down below. Lodge members' wives served refreshments. People paid for the dancing; then they paid extra for the supper.

There were ice-cream socials, usually on the lawn of somebody's ranch. They did it to raise money for the lodges, clubs, one thing and another.

People that had cows and had rich cream agreed to bring the ice cream. We don't have the same kind of nice rich cream they had in those days, unless you have somebody on a ranch that can sell you separated cream. Where they got the ice was another thing. When I was a little girl, they didn't have this lake down here. After the lake was put in, it was so easy to get ice. One of the men had ice saws and equipment; they'd cut out the ice and help one another load. I don't know when that started. They must have been able to put ice away, or they couldn't have had ice-cream socials. Off some of the creeks, maybe.

They made good cakes to go with the ice cream. That's where a lot of the recipes got scattered out. When they'd bring something that was real nice, they'd be asked for the recipe; then other families had it, too. Anybody that didn't give out a recipe was peculiar.

When I was about twelve, my mother turned me loose in the kitchen. She said to read the recipe and follow it. I can remember my mother said, "You must be real careful not to waste anything." And my grandmother said to me, "Don't waste food, because remember, somebody, somewhere in the world is hungry."

After a courtship of "maybe two years," Winifred married Fayette Jeffers when she was "almost twenty-three." The wedding was held in the Episcopal church in Jeffers.

I'd always known Faye. He lived just across the river [in Jeffers]. He'd been away to school quite a bit.

We had an early morning wedding because we were going to get in the car and go up to the edge of Hebgen Lake, where several of his family and some friends had a hunting camp. That's where we were going for our wedding trip, and into Yellowstone Park.

We had a wedding breakfast on the way to the camp. We cooked bacon and eggs and fried some potatoes along the Madison River. His family followed us up there. Then they came back, and we went on.

They were beginning to use cars [in Yellowstone Park], and there were quite a number of people there. They're wearing it out now.

The young couple's first home was on a ranch up on Jack Creek.

It wasn't a very big house, a frame house; we had to build onto it. I guess it's still up there. We got water out of Jack Creek, not very far from the house. We heated with woodstoves, two heating stoves, and a combination [wood and coal] cookstove. We had no electricity, no running water, just a makeshift kitchen. A makeshift kitchen takes more steps than one that was really planned.

You had to have a place for the water. Water bucket sittin' there. There was a reservoir and a warming oven on the stove. I had an ordinary sink; it held two dishpans. We had a plumber come in and put in a septic tank, and drain the sink into the tank. It wasn't anything fancy, but it was a big help.

Winifred described the household chores she would and would not do as a newlywed.

No sir, I would not haul water! That's one thing I objected to. I could in a pinch, and I wasn't lazy, but I wasn't going to establish the habit.

I felt like I was stumbling along, but I knew enough about cooking and cleaning up and things like that to get by. With common intelligence I think you can manage to make a schedule for yourself. You have to.

We always had dry wood for starting fires. I preferred dried fir. It seemed to have the greatest heat. Indeed, I did not split my own wood. I could do it, though. As a matter of fact, I've always loved to split wood, but when I was married, I certainly expected to have the wood brought in, and I expected to have the water brought in.

Cooking on those stoves was not easy. There are so many drafts on it. You shut everything up fairly tight, and then there's a space to move the pot or kettle back so it isn't on the direct heat. So it gets a mild heat and simmers. You have to learn; it gets to be a habit.

You had to learn when the oven was at the right temperature. At first when I learned, I put my hand in the oven and counted. I can't remember the number of counts that I had, getting hot on the top of my hand. I could tell when it was ready for a cake. Most always it worked. When I got my cookstove, it had a thermostat on the front.

Maintaining the right temperature became a habit. You had a good bed of coals, and then you know how much firewood to put on. If you wanted to get a quick fire, you put on some kindling. I baked a lot of bread that way.

Cleaning the stove was a lot of work. There's a place to take the ashes off where the heat from the firebox had gone across the top of the oven. It dropped some ashes there. You could scrape all that off; it would fall down to the side. You opened the door below the oven, reached in with a little hoe, and got all those ashes out to make a free circulation of air. That was the hardest part of cleaning the stove. Underneath the firebox was a thing that caught the ashes. You cleaned the stove every day. The oven didn't have to be cleaned but once a week.

We put ashes on the trash pile. Never did use 'em. About once or twice a year we cleaned stovepipes, whether they needed it or not.

One of Winifred's busiest times of year was threshing time, when she had to feed the threshing crew.

When threshing time came, that was a problem. Houses weren't big enough to accommodate all the men that would come with the threshing machines. We had to set up tables, and we had benches we could bring. The farm wives used to help one another.

You had to have plenty of meat. Usually we had a roast or a lot of boiling meat for the noon meal and potatoes and gravy and a vegetable. It's the time of year when you have cabbage or lettuce that you could have for a salad. You always had to have fruit and cake for supper, but for the noon meal you must have PIE!

I would say you'd have twelve or more men [to feed]. Some of the ranchers went home because they had to milk cows, but they always helped one another during the day. Oftentimes after they milked in the morning, they came for breakfast. That kept their wives from having to get up and get breakfast.

The biggest meal was at noon. You could have cold meat for supper, but you must have a good hot meal at noon, and plenty of it. The men always ate first, and the women waited table. And furnished lots of coffee.

If you ever did run out of food, you borrowed from a neighbor who might be two or three miles away. But believe me, they were always good about helping you out.

Occasionally, the family would get "rained in" with the threshers.

Most all of the men who came with a machine had someplace to go that wasn't too far away. If it stormed too much, they would estimate how many days it would take before they could start up again. They'd just take off and go home. That's the advantage of farmers helping farmers.

Winifred made use of the bounty in her garden.

I canned a lot of stuff out of the garden. I always had good luck with my canning because I cooked it more than it said in the books. Because of the altitude, you know. Canned a lot of fruit, made jellies and jams. We had strawberries, chokecherries, huckleberries in the mountains. I've gone huckleberrying way up to West Yellowstone. You're fortunate to be able to get any. As soon as people find out there's a patch, they're there. It's such a choice fruit. And of course we had peaches to can.

I've canned meat, wild meat, too. It's just boiled meat when you take it out. I think it spoils the flavor to can it. It's better than nothing, that's all I'd say.

Chicken cans very well. I raised chickens, turkeys, too. I bought them as chicks for both meat and eggs. I never did care for too many chickens. Turkeys had more sense than chickens. If you're careful of them when they're little things, so they don't get wet or cold, they get hardy. My turkeys, I used to whistle for them, and they'd come from away off. You couldn't get a chicken to do that.

I guess I must've made pets of my turkeys. I didn't intend to. It's hard to dispose of a pet. You can't bear the thought of killing them, and you don't want to sell them.

I tried not to make pets of any particular turkey, but I did have a little pet turkey one time. It was so sickly, and I doctored it, and it got to be fairly sturdy. It would hang around me, around my feet. I had to kind of break it from doing that.

We had a basement under the house at the ranch. We had potatoes down there, and it kept them very well. I had shelves for all my canned goods. We stored carrots, rutabagas, and potatoes. We tried different ways of storing. Sometimes I think they were better off just to be in the dry bin. If you put them on anything moist, they'd rot.

Winifred had a definite opinion on her role in the butchering process.

The butchering process? Oh, dear, I didn't ever watch it! I know they had to shoot the animal, then put it on a hoist, lift it up so they could take out its insides. I never helped to skin or take out an animal's insides. I've been hunting and killed a deer. I don't actually know how you cut them open, but I know you have to get all the insides out of them and cool the meat.

Another chore Winifred chose not to learn was milking.

I never could stay with it long enough to milk a cow. My hands weren't accustomed to it, I guess. I had big enough hands, but I had never milked, and I didn't learn. I could get a little milk. I never did learn how to do stripping. That's when you're through milking, when you get most of the cream. I knew I'd have to do it if I learned.

We sold our cream. And we had a separator. It was hand-run. Washing the separator was part of my job. Everybody dreaded that. You'd use a lot of cold water first [to clean the discs], then you'd use tepid water. After that, you'd put them in hot soapy water, scald them, and air-dry them.

I churned once in a great while. I had a barrel churn, one of those things that went back and forth. I didn't mind that at all. I'd helped my grandmother do it so much, I sort of liked it. I imagine you could put in two gallons at a time. I never made any great batches of butter, only a small batch. A lot of people used eggbeaters to make a little bit of butter. I had helped my grandmother with her churning lots of times when I was a little girl, but she always had it about ready to be butter when I took ahold of it.

How long it took depended on the age of the cream. If you stirred your cream a little bit when you were adding new cream, stirred the cream in the crock, it churned a lot quicker than if you were careless about it. You kept it mixed all the time. I made butter into pound blocks. I still have my wooden form. We used almost all butter in cooking. It tastes wonderful. That was the fat you used in cakes and cookies. I thought it was a great blessing, though, when Crisco came on the market. It seemed like it creamed easier than butter did.

I had a bin table called a Kitchen Queen. One bin held sugar, the other flour. It had a lot of area on top.

We sold our wheat and bought flour, but there was a place in Sheridan [Montana] where you could have flour made if you wanted to take your own wheat over there. We never did.

I would buy only about fifty pounds of flour at a time. That's all my cabinet would hold.

I baked a lot of bread. I had an everlasting yeast. That's a wonderful thing. My cousin got it in Butte, made bread with it, and found out it was so nice. She sent me a quart by parcel post. You keep it alive by putting potato water with it, then make up your yeast. Be sure to have plenty of liquid. The next day, pour that back into the receptacle and put it in the refrigerator. In five days, maybe less, if you want to make bread, use that for a starter. It made wonderful bread.

After I came down here [to Ennis from the ranch], I lost it. My starter wasn't as good as it had been. I guess I didn't make bread often enough. Up on the ranch, I made bread more often and renewed [the starter]. I baked about every four days, six loaves at a time. I think I baked whenever I ran out of bread. I had to plan ahead a little bit, though, because there'd be something coming up, that I couldn't spend all that extra time. It took three to four hours to devote to the bread.

My mother got an automatic bread mixer for me. It had some kind of arm on it. You'd crank it, and it would stir the bread up after it had been made thick enough to work down. I never felt like it did a good job, so I used to turn it out on the board and work it. You can tell by the feel [of the dough] when you've worked it and kneaded it enough. I don't think I could do it now; I've lost the touch.

I didn't have much spare time, not very much. You might have it at night after the children went to bed. Then you could sit down and read something. Bedtime was by nine. Pret' near had to [be] to get any rest to do a day's work.

The day started about half past five. I was supposed to have breakfast ready when milking was done. Fixing breakfast entailed cooking meat and eggs, ham or bacon for the meat. Then you'd have to have toast or pancakes, muffins, some kind of hot bread. Men had to have a big breakfast; they were supposed to work until noon. Then, in the wintertime, they had to go feed the cattle.

The noon meal at twelve o'clock was the biggest meal of the day. I spent my mornings getting ready for *that*. If you had pie, you had to be baking pie. A farmer's life is not an easy life.

We had no running water nor electricity. You didn't have cake mixes in those days; you didn't have pancake mixes. But you did have sourdough. Laundry had to wait until everything else was out of the way. After you had finished breakfast and cleared it away, and before you started dinner. Usually you had a heavy meal at noon—meat and potatoes, vegetable, pie, some pudding, something like that—a lighter meal at supper. Supper was a more relaxed meal. You could serve cold dishes. If you didn't have cold meat, you'd have to have something fried. You had fruit and possibly cake for dessert.

I did laundry at least once a week, maybe small things in the middle of the week. When the children were small, I did laundry every single day. You have to. They were fifteen months apart. My first was a boy; my second was a girl. I had a Maytag. It had a gasoline motor. My mother supplied that, and it certainly was a great help. I didn't have a washhouse. I just had a porch.

In those days, Madison Lake, which had been formed twelve years before Winifred was married, was the source of ice for the neighborhood icehouses.

The farmers used to go down there in a body and cut the ice, bring it home, and put it in the icehouse. Cutting depended entirely on the season. It could be as early as just before Christmas; it could be after Christmas. They cut when the river gorged and when it was cold enough.

They had a horse that dragged some kind of machine that marked it off, then they sawed it with handsaws. They hauled it from the lake in squares and put the squares together on the bottom of the icehouse, and what little space there was left between them, they chopped up other ice real fine, poked it down with a shingle and hoped it would freeze together. After they got a whole layer built, they put a lot of sawdust over it and put another layer of ice on top. I think they must have allowed three or four feet of sawdust around the outside edges, and the floor of the icehouse had sawdust on it.

It'd keep all summer. The icehouse had plenty of ventilation. There were ventilators at each end. Each man had his own icehouse. If you had a cow, you were expected to have an icehouse so you could have ice cream.

We made ice cream quite often. I expect maybe once a week. It didn't seem it took very long. You had to get [fresh] ice out of the refrigerator anyway. I made ice cream with cream and sugar, some milk, and then I got a recipe that had raw eggs in it. I beat up the eggs and put them and the flavoring in. That's all there was to it. Some people made a custard. They made a custard with the milk and eggs, put in the vanilla.

My husband did the cranking. I helped to put in the ice to pack it, that sort of thing, to get it going. While he was cranking, lots of times I'd keep filling it in with ice and salt.

We had three different sizes of ice cream freezers. We had a little two-quart that I had before we got married, and then we had a three-quart and a four-quart.

I usually made vanilla, but I have a lot of recipes, good ones. I've tried all of them. I've made chocolate, I've made caramel, and I've made fresh peach ice cream, strawberry ice cream. I've got all the recipes in my book. I have some recipes for sauce, too. But ice cream was enough. Rich enough without putting a sauce on top. Made with good cream.

Winifred's grandfather, mother, and Winifred herself served as postmaster in Ennis for a total of eighty-six years.

The post office used to be the gathering place. It was in our general store until it got so big they moved it and built a building for it. After I retired, they still had the post office in that building where the Nearly New Store and the Tackle Shop are.

Three generations of us were postmaster: My grand-father, from the time the post office was instituted [1881] until he died in 1898. My mother succeeded him [1898–1940], and then I succeeded her [1940–67]. You know everybody that comes in after their mail. There are so many more people here since I got out of the post office, a lot of people I don't know. But they may know me, because I'm about the oldest woman in town.

A person remembers a lot of things from when they were young; they pick up things as they go along. I think they are wiser as they get older. Things that are so important to you when you're young are not so important when you're older. It was important to get to see a lot of new things or to go to new places and all that. Now I don't have the energy. I'm perfectly satisfied to read about it now. I read what's in the papers, and sometimes I listen to the TV, but I don't make it a habit. There's lots to read. Since I've had eye trouble, I've gotten behind a whole lot with my reading.

I'm ninety-one. I think I've lived longer than any-body ever thought I would, longer than I ever thought I'd live. I know my days are numbered; I just don't know the number. What's the use to worry about it?

Winifred Jeffers was interviewed at her home in Ennis in December 1986. She died in Ennis at age ninety-four on July 2, 1990.

CLARA PETERSON NICKELSON

". . . the land was there, ready for homesteading, free, from the government."

Clara Peterson Nickelson's parents were both Scandinavian immigrants, as evidenced by Clara's slight accent and precise manner of speaking. She was a heavy woman and plain, with thin graying hair. She was born in Park County, Montana, on June 19, 1905, the youngest of four children. Her mother had emigrated from Norway as a young girl still in her teens.

A great many young people emigrated at the same time; it was the thing to do. They had a good time because there were a lot of people who knew each other. The ship was overly crowded, and when the seas got stormy, sickness overcame them. It was a long and tedious journey. I do not know how long it took, but it was slow.

She went to Minnesota. I'm not sure why she stopped in Minnesota, but I think her biggest reason for leaving was in the aftermath of a bad electrical storm, tornado-type. Looking for better weather, she came to Montana, where she had a brother who met her in Livingston. She worked as a maid in homes.

My father was born in Sweden. I don't know much about his family or what they did. He emigrated as a young man because of the excitement of going to the new land. He first went to a port in Canada, then later came into the States. He kept coming west and eventually stayed in Park County. He found employment in the coal mines in the vicinity.

My parents were married in Cokedale, Montana, in 1895 or 1896, when the mines were producing coal and coke. About fifteen hundred people lived in the mining camp where there now is nothing.

After the mines were closed down, in three or four years, he homesteaded and tried ranching. It was a homestead near the mountains, quite high, but very good soil. A lot of timber needed to be cut and the land reclaimed. It produced a satisfactory living for many years.

Starting as those people did—and there were many of them from the mines who had absolutely nothing to begin ranching with—[was hard] but the land was there, ready for homesteading, free, from the government. One hundred sixty acres if they could prove some sort of habitation and that some part of their living came from the land; I believe it was three years. [The Homestead Act of 1862 called for a five-year "prove-up" period.] With the help of people who would testify that they had lived on the land, had produced on the land—to satisfy the rules from the government—they were given a deed to those 160 acres.

And a lot of it that was given was placed on the paper in Washington and really should not ever have been expected to be homesteaded. Location, soil, whatever was on the land, how some of it would be steep mountainsides full of trees. Perhaps it didn't show on the maps in the offices of Washington.

I do not remember the original house my family lived in, but as soon as he was able, my father cut logs and built a log house, which was very comfortable to live in. It consisted of a kitchen and dining room, three bedrooms, and another little room that eventually was made into a bathroom. A one-story house heated by woodstoves.

The kitchen was large, big enough for a family table, for the family to eat their meals. The dining room table was used only for special occasions. The range provided enough heat for the kitchen. There was a pantry adjacent to the kitchen, and there was what we called the spring-house, a room where a concrete tank had water flowing in and out from a very cold spring which provided the refrigeration for cream, milk, and other things. Water was piped in very soon after the house was built, piped from the spring into the sink. It was all gravity flow.

The problem with the running water was the lime and the minerals, locally known as "very hard water." The so-called water font that was put in the stove would build up with lime and was not satisfactory. In lieu of a manufactured water font, my father instituted a series of pipes that could be removed and replaced in the firebox to heat the water as it went through.

It was a wood-burning stove. We did not have coal; it would have to be hauled in. Wood was so plentiful we used it for the kitchen stove and also in the heater in the dining-living room.

Some families chose homestead land, sight unseen, and had to make the best of it.

You took what was available. The area there where my father had his homestead at one time had a dozen or more homesteads. The little school that was built and provided schooling for those homesteaders' kids at one time had ten or twelve students. Now there are none. The school has been closed for many, many years.

Some people settled up in the mountains instead of down on the valley floor. Partly because the soil had that extra depth and quality to it. The valley soil was sandy. It was closer to town than some of the places down by the river.

The mountains also received more rainfall. If you were dependent on rain, and that was the only thing they knew, it made quite a lot of difference. The irrigating was not anything my father knew about. It was all dry-land farming up there. There wasn't any irrigating yet.

It took a lot of hard work, and a lot of capital, and it also found all these people with no machinery, nor horses, no nothing. It took years, it took *years* of plowing by hand to start with, then to teams, and at the very end, the very, very end, some of the small tractors got into that area.

Some homesteading families lost the determination to remain on their land.

Those who stayed after the land was proved up would buy out their neighbors. Some families, as each person in the family was twenty-one years old, would file on a homestead of his own. Some of these made a compact land of five or six homesteads. It is all grazing now, every bit of it. There is nobody living in that entire area, making anything from the land.

It was a very pleasant place to live, situated at the head of Strickland Crick, a tributary to the Yellowstone River, about fourteen miles from Livingston.

The difference between living there then and living there now is that now we would consider it isolated and too small. It is better suited to grazing. It has gone back to grazing land. It would be better if it had not been plowed in the first place.

In Clara's day, every child in the family had chores to do. By the time a child was in the first or second grade, he or she would know how to milk.

Mother made cheese for our own consumption and occasionally would sell some. We would save the entire output from one milking, put it in a large washtub-type vat, and by the use of rennet would solidify the milk or set it. Then it could be sliced, and the whey would come to the surface. That would all have to be put in cheesecloth sacks and put into a cheese press, which was a little container with a screw top. The screw was constantly turned down to squeeze it tighter and squeeze the buttermilk out.

It would take a week or ten days before the cheese could be taken out, and it would hold its shape. A crust formed on the outside, a little salt was rubbed in, and the cheese would be left to dry and ripen in the sun.

We liked it when it was new. The newer cheeses are more soft and malleable. The later, sharp cheese gets sort of crumbly. The cheese was white unless you used the yellow tablet of color in the milk.

A lot of things were made by loving hands at home.

Those women did an awful lot of handwork, an awful lot of braiding for rugs, making this and making that. It wasn't a tedious life, and it was not hardship. We never thought of it as hardship.

We all had our small chores when we were youngsters. Gathering eggs or taking scraps, feeding chickens. That sort of thing. And gathering cows for milking. That was a very early day chore because they would be off up in the pasture and would have to be gone after, brought in. It was for the most part fun. Always there would be one or two [cow] bells so that you had a pretty good idea where they were. And they were glad to get in to get milked. With the dog to help, it was a short job.

You had to learn to get along with the chickens. I suppose there were quite a few pecks [while taking eggs from the nest]. We didn't have incubators, not while I was a child. We raised our chickens from hens, so that was another chore. Each hen takes just a little extra care while she's incubating her eggs and hatching. They have to be watched, to be fed.

I didn't like to cook, so I managed to get out of that as much as I could. I really didn't know too much about it except for the more simple things. My sisters did better; they were both older. That was just fine, I got by.

I preferred outside work. I was able to help with the harvesting. I was able to help hay and drive the horses, all that sort of thing.

I still remember my father's haying methods. The first was a very simple wagon and pitchfork. I suppose he cut some fields with a scythe [at first], but a very simple mower was early on the scene, pulled with two horses. And then they had a rake to go with it, to rake the hay into windrows. The haycocks, or shocks, were put up by hand with pitchfork, pitched onto a hayrack to bring to the barn [to be stacked].

My father built a log barn when I was just a little child. He had quite a large loft room in the barn to store hay for the milk cows and for the horses. [One method for stacking the hay up in the loft] was to get a track the length of the barn with rope and pulleys on one end [hanging from a beam outside the upper loft door], with a fork that would go down into the hay and take a whole quantity. [Through the doors] at the other end of the barn was the same rope with the same pulleys hitched to a team that would pull all of that up, ride it on the tracks through the barn, and dump it wherever you wanted it to be dumped.

Driving the stacker team was always the youngest child's job. But you must do it *correctly!* You must do it with the right amount of speed so that the fork would go down into the hay and pick up a load. Or, sometimes people had slings that would be put on the bottom of the hayrack and another sling on top, and those would be brought together and hitched onto a pulley arrangement. The slings had a trip that would open them at the bottom, drop the hay out. And that worked pretty good.

[A later method] was the stackers, the overhead stackers. [A team of horses also pulled these overhead stackers, and when the trip was thrown, the stacker would catapult the hay up into the hayloft.] They're still used in some places. The stacker had to have the buck rake to go with it. Some people were ingenious enough to practically put a buck rake together on their own. Otherwise, they were purchased. Little by little new machinery was acquired.

Machinery was important, but of more importance was always the raising of their own food.

Staples would have to be purchased: flour, sugar, beans—navy beans, lima beans, kidney beans—canned goods that one was unable to can. We never canned peas, even after they had the ways of doing them. We were afraid of the home-canned not being quite secure. Tomatoes, we had a great many cans of tomatoes. They were really a tremendous standby. Though perhaps they didn't realize it, we know now that it was a good source of vitamin C.

There were other things that had to be purchased at the store whenever a trip was made, but that didn't happen so very often. The dried yeast, of course, would keep for the bread. Oranges and apples would be almost the only kind of fruit. Grapefruit was not known at that time.

Fruits were usually cooked. A lot of applesauce was canned in the fall in glass jars. Peaches were canned, too, except for all of these dried peaches, dried fruits that were bought.

We weren't able to raise any kind of fruit ourselves. Nothing, no apples, no anything. Fruit had to be bought fresh.

Cabbages were put away for the winter. Cauliflower didn't do so well, but cabbages did quite well. And, of course, potatoes. No potatoes were ever purchased. Carrots and rutabagas would keep reasonably well. Onions, we always had onions. Turnips, I don't remember turnips keeping. I think they were strictly summertime fare.

Winter vegetables were stored in the cellar. Every ranch had its own [root] cellar in those days, dug into a hillside. The deeper they went, the better the quality of moisture and temperature. It was great on a hot summer day, it was cool; on a cold winter day, it was warm. And everything smells good.

We had currants, currant bushes, but they all went for jelly. Rhubarb. That can be canned, too, and with strawberries, would make good jam. In the latter years we raised strawberries. We didn't when I was small. That was something we tried later. But they did well. One crop, not everbearing.

My family raised cattle and sold the calves. Today, it takes a much larger herd, it seems, than it did in those days. Even just a few were apparently sufficient to provide for the tax money and a few other essentials. And we had horses, draft horses and some saddle horses. Sometimes the same ones had to work for both. We always had at least two or three saddle horses.

Once in a while we'd get a few bum lambs in the spring and raise some sheep. Chickens. We always had chickens, so we had our own eggs.

We had our own beef and our own pork. Of course, that meant the preservation of beef, with beef all through the winter. Fresh beef had to be purchased on those trips to town. In the spring and the summer, it was just hams and bacon, and they got pretty old. Of course, as the spring chickens grew, and an occasional lamb . . . but nothing could be kept too long. No fresh meat could be kept too long without refrigeration, and that was true even for the city people in those days. Unless you had access to the market, you had to do with the preserved meats. Baloney, a lot of baloney. I don't remember whether wieners were used. I think I was a fairly good-sized child before I knew what a wiener was.

We never did beef [in the smokehouse], just pork. I didn't like the smokehouse much, so I didn't bother about being interested in what was going on in that smoky place. The butchering took place when the pigs were the right age, late fall, early winter.

I don't know how long the smoking process took, but it was just by chance that they managed to get it right. You'd have to be pretty careful with a ham after you cut into it. Keeping it secure and away from flies were the biggest problems. Ham was kept in the spring-house, carefully wrapped in lots of cheesecloth, and kept cool. The water in the springhouse was cool enough that hams immersed in it would keep for quite a long time. That water was really cold, forty degrees, perhaps, but it was a problem without refrigeration.

A lot of people buried their hams in the granary, under wheat or sawdust. I think the reason for that was to keep [them] away from flies and insects. I don't know that it was really the best idea, but I know it was done quite a lot.

Hams would have to be precooked in cold water and brought to a boil. Then the water would be disposed of because it would carry quite a lot of salt. It was the salt that preserved, as much as the smoke. And it was too salty for frying if it were not preboiled. In boiling a ham, the water could be changed two or three times. It would lose a great deal of the salt that way.

The major meal of the day was after school. An early supper. When school was in, we took our lunch, and we were always hungry when school was out. [Supper . . .] oh, meat, potatoes, gravy, vegetable. Much the same as we find in any country home today. Probably a lot more heavy desserts than we serve today. Pies were used a great deal. Puddings. Nearly always there were cookies or cake or something.

I can remember being quite a grown person before we had packages that made the new dessert we call Jell-O. Before that we had gelatin. One typical fruit dish would be to combine some of all the dried fruits with some tapioca and gelatin and sugar and make what we called a fruit soup. It is Scandinavian, one of my mother's carryovers. It was served as a pudding, along with cream. Whipped cream, usually. It was good; it was very good. That was before tapioca was modernized, those big "fish eyes" as we called them. They were good, but they took longer to cook.

There was also a product at that time that Mother bought in boxes. Seemed that she had quite good-sized boxes. They called it Sego—S-E-G-O, and that's very much the same as our modern tapioca. I don't know whether there is such a product on the market now. I haven't thought of it in years. Mother used it all by itself for puddings as we do our custard tapioca puddings now.

My family kept quite a few Scandinavian Christmas traditions, as many as were adaptable. Like, oh, Christmas breakfast, there had to be the particular kind of roll that fit with Christmas, baked only at that time of the year. The kringle, we called them. It would be lighter than most bread and made into a circular shape and frosted and trimmed with a little decoration that belonged with Christmas.

The Christmas baking went on for weeks, for months before the holiday. All manner of cookies, fancy breads, sweet breads. Regular breads, rye breads, sesame breads. As a rule, a great deal of caraway with the rye. And there were the fruits; they had the dried fruits.

At Christmas there was always lutefisk, which is a far cry from what we go to the market and buy today. The only lutefisk on the market was the original dry product. They would be very small, narrow pieces of elongated fish. The entire fish, which would be two, two and a half feet long, was dried 'til it was barely a two-inch width. Then Mother would have to start the luting process.

Luting consisted of immersing the fish and soaking it for the necessary time. You had to judge how [much] time it needed in a solution of either wood ashes and water or lye and water, until it soaked up and grew to its original width of four to five inches. Until it had just the right look to it. Then it would be renewed and washed in cold water and prepared, usually in a net or a cheesecloth bag dipped in boiling water. The tail is usually taken off, the head cut off. Cut to make it more convenient, [then cooked] by putting it in that cheese-cloth bag and boiling it.

It is served with butter and cream sauce. Today we buy it in its prepared state, and all that is necessary is to boil it or bake it. Some of it is deboned, some of it isn't. It's a main dish, served with potatoes at Christmas, New Year's. And that is about the only time of the year. Really, even yet, you do not see the freshly prepared lutefisk in the market except in December. Not many stores carry it.

We always had a Christmas tree, we always had the lighted candles, and of course those were the American customs. They were adopted; they were not the tradition from Scandinavian countries.

We had lighted candles on the tree. We never had a fire, but my mother was always very much afraid of it. As children, we didn't see where there could be that much danger. We watched our candles. There were no boughten trimmings on the tree. There were little circles of construction paper, which we brought home from school, red and yellow and green. Little circles and chains, strung across [the tree]. Also, maybe some little objects, angels or animals, that we had done at school.

We went to town once a week, or once every two weeks to the creamer's. That would be about as long as the cream would stay good. We had two creameries then, the Livingston Creamery and the Farmer's Creamery.

The custom at the grocery was to pay once a year. We never thought of doing it differently. Just kept a bill running until cattle or produce were sold. And then we paid the grocery bill.

It was Blakeslee Grocery Store, as long as I can remember. I'm pretty sure all he had was groceries. Of course, nobody went and picked anything off the shelf. You stood at the counter and ordered, and the grocer wrote it down and made up the order. Always there was a chair or someplace to sit. Folks sat and visited—more than one chair—in the front. Kind of a gathering place, really, the grocery stores were.

When we went to town, most of the time [we ate] at the Chinese Café, and for a quarter you had a marvelous meal. Several choices: good soups, homemade noodles, good things. A nice place, very neat and clean. I think they were right along the middle of Main Street.

When we were old enough to go to high school, we had to come to town, of course, to stay. There were a lot of people that were looking for girls particularly. They called it "work for your board and room." There would be small tasks, babysitting, that type of thing. We did that part of the time. Part of the time, my sister being quite a little older, we had a little rented place and she cooked, she took care of us younger children. We all went to school [in town], even grade school then, because we didn't always manage to have [a teacher for the country school].

As people moved out, one by one, we got less and less people, and finally had to quit having school. Changing population does that to the schools.

[In high school] we had domestic science—cooking and sewing. I took as little as I possibly could, and I really don't remember much about cooking or the sewing, either one. And I was not required to take as much as some people took because we had the normal training at that time, and it eliminated a lot of subjects. We didn't have to have that many credits in domestic science to graduate. We took enough of the basics to have credits for graduation, but we had also those extra credits in psychology, methods of teaching, penmanship, teaching of penmanship, that type of thing. I can't remember what else. I know we had to sacrifice physics, and that didn't bother me.

When I took the normal training, it led to special certificates in addition to my high school diploma, like a second-grade teaching certificate, good for any rural school, good for two years. And then after two years, we could go back and we could go to Normal [college] and pick up a few credits and first-grade certificate. By continuing, which a lot of the girls did, they could finally get to where they had a life certificate.

I was disenchanted completely with the Normal School. In the first place, I hated to spend the money I'd worked so hard to gain, and then I had to take the same subjects that I had had [with] a much, much better, more individualized teaching of in high school. I didn't go back. I had my first-grade certificate; when it expired, I let it go.

I believe it could be renewed once with so many months of teaching under it. I felt I almost wasted my time because I had had the same subject matter before. I got good grades. I got better grades than I did in high school, but I didn't study one lickin' bit. I had already had a better course!

The first fall that I graduated from high school, I taught back at that little school at Cokedale, where my folks were married. There were only a very few children, but they had some money, and they wanted to have school as long as their money lasted. They started early to avoid the fuel [costs] as much as possible. Our school began the first of August, and we were through the last of January, early February. [When] I took my reports to the county superintendent [of schools], she asked me if I would finish the term at Cooke City [a small community in the mountains near the northeast entrance to Yellowstone National Park]. The teacher there had not come back from her vacation at Christmas. Going up to Cooke City in the wintertime was an interesting experience because nobody at that time used motor vehicles in the winter, and there was no public conveyance by road from Livingston. I went by train from Livingston to Gardiner; then in the morning I went by the Cooke City Stage, which was the Shaw and Powell Stage to Cooke City. That took two and a half more days. The first day we started with a spring wagon and four horses, and about six or seven miles out of Gardiner we transferred to a bobsled with four horses. The driver had to unload his wagon, all the materials, onto the bobsled, and that included my trunk, which I should never have taken, filled with books, plus groceries for the store and other incidentals for people in Cooke City. We proceeded on to Yancey's, which was a Shaw and Powell stage at the location of what is now Camp Roosevelt [in Yellowstone National Park]. The next day we went on and stopped at Soda Butte Station where there is nothing now, but at that time there was a good little barn and a nice station for overnight. The next day we got to Cooke City.

I had not too many—I think about eight children in school—but I had both the seventh and eighth grades, and that meant that those people had to pass their state examinations. The seventh grade had two subjects, physiology and geography. The eighth graders had all the rest of the subjects. The seventh graders couldn't enter eighth grade without a satisfactory passing grade, and the eighth graders could not go to high school without having a passing grade on the state examinations.

We had lots of things we did for fun. We could ski, we could sleigh. If the roads were snowy and cold, they would always take us to school in the sled with the horses, and that was fun. Simple things were fun.

Summer was fun, but it was, I suppose, lonely. I don't know. We didn't think about being lonely. You didn't think of anything different, 'twas all. I think my father [was] irked, more than any of us. I think his early itchiness to go places and do things were still with him, but impossible. There was no way to do it.

Money was so entirely different. A quarter bought a pair of shoes. The children's shoes didn't cost more than a quarter. The stores had quantities of material for clothes, and all of the children's clothing was handmade. Practically all of it. Coats, perhaps, had to be purchased. But there was a little money saved from this and from that. They were thrifty!

There were very few divorces, very few. I've wondered exactly why. I suppose you could find all manner of reasons. Maybe people simply made up their minds to grin and bear it. Maybe they never considered anything different.

Better or worse, I'm sure I don't know; I don't know.

It seems strange that the land and the people could have changed so much in just a generation's time, but there are a great many people living today who remember these same things.

It certainly was a different time.

Clara Nickelson was interviewed at her home in Livingston in May 1983. She died in Livingston in November 1995. She was ninety years old.

EVA EYMAN DEPUY

"I bet my mother wished they hadn't come."

Born on January 16, 1905, Eva Eyman DePuy lived all of her life near Livingston, Montana. She was a tall woman, forthright, with a good sense of humor. She loved animals, especially horses, and you could tell from one glance at her hands that she had spent many hours in the out-of-doors. She was nearly blind at the time of the interview, but she had once been a voracious reader. Now she was given to returning in her imagination to enjoy again the books she had once read.

Her parents, both natives of Ohio, had lived in Indiana and then Iowa before coming came to Montana in 1893. With their three young children, they homesteaded up the Shields River in Park County.

The West was building up, and they came, well, sort of, for my father's health. I bet my mother wished they hadn't come. But they stuck it out.

They lived in a little cabin that could have been a trapper's cabin. They all lived in it one winter. [My mother] brought her mother with her because her father had died. [Parents, grandmother,] and three children in that small cabin. Ah, I don't see how they did it. I don't think it ever did have a floor. When I first knew that little cabin, they were using it for a blacksmith's shop. It had a forge in there and such like.

The homestead cabin my father built down over the hill from it did have a floor. It was boards put together, and there were cracks. They had a rag carpet that they used to put on the floor in the living room part. Every spring we took that up, took it outside, and beat it. Then it had to go back in again, go out, and come in again in the fall. They put newspapers and such underneath the carpet for warmth.

Eva's maternal grandmother, who lived with the family in the first little cabin, died before Eva was born in 1905. Later, her Uncle John Eyman and his family came to live nearby. Arriving with them were the Eyman grandparents. Grandmother Eyman lived with the John Eymans and Grandpa Eyman lived with Eva's family, which had expanded to include eight children.

We had Grandpa with us until he died. I was eighteen months old; I barely remember him. I can remember going to his bedroom door, but I couldn't go in because he was sick. He had cancer. I used to go look in, and he'd talk to me. My brothers and sisters say I couldn't remember that, but I do.

I'll tell you what happened. They got a big tent, and they built a platform to put it on. My two older brothers and a sister or two had to sleep in the tent in the wintertime. You think back on that, and you wonder, "How on earth?" I think they had a stove, but it was pretty cold. Every night they'd go to bed, they took two sets of flatirons, heated up on the kitchen stove, wrapped in towels. The girls took one set, the boys the other, to put in their beds. That's the way they kept warm. But it was pretty rugged.

My father brought logs from the Crazy Mountains in the hope of building a new house. After a year or so, they got busy and put up this other house, which had four bedrooms upstairs and one downstairs, a living room, a dining room, and a kitchen. It seemed like heaven.

Eva's mother delivered her babies at home, most of them with the help of a neighborhood midwife, Grandma Adams.

Everybody called her Grandma Adams. When I was born—I'm the eighth of a family of nine—my mother had quite a bit of trouble. Maybe I came too soon, I don't know. My father went to get Grandma Adams, and the boys went to get my aunt who lived not too far away. She came, and I guess everything was taken care of before Grandma Adams got there. That's what they tell me.

But it was a different story when my youngest brother was born. I remember that night vividly. There was no telephone. They had to have gone way over on the Shields River somewhere to find a telephone.

Anyway, the doctor did come from Livingston. Sixteen miles.

My mother must have had a lot of courage. When they first homesteaded, well, the first few years there couldn't have been much of a way to farm to make a living. My dad worked around, doing carpenter work.

They came out here in one of those emigrant cars. They brought everything they owned. Mom and the three children rode in the passenger car, but Dad stayed with the stock. They brought the milk cow, and there were three horses, a team and a mare that had a colt the next spring. Oh, chickens, all their furniture, farming equipment. I think about how they managed; I marvel at what they did.

Just as soon as we were able, we all had chores to do. We helped around the house, and we also milked cows.

I can't remember being instructed at all. We learned by watching. It was expected of us, and we didn't object. In later years, we didn't want hired men around, so we did boys' work quite a bit.

Us girls, we had our own horses that we took care of, and we didn't want these men around the barn. We wanted a free hand. We helped with the cows, and we also helped out in the field with the haying. Some of the neighbors thought Dad was mean, but it wasn't his choice; it was ours. We got a kick out of [haying]. We did it with horses.

My older brothers cut the hay with a horse-drawn mower with a sickle blade. Then it was raked with a dump rake. You went along with this rake—you've surely seen those things sitting in fields—teeth that are shaped like this, and when they're catching up the hay they're down, but when you want to dump the hay, you have a lever that you pulled, and that dumped it. Then you went on and gathered up some more. Obsolete now, but there's a few of them around.

An older brother, he was out in the field, he and my dad, and they pitched the hay onto flat sleds. Two of us girls and my younger brother drove the teams [that pulled the sleds] to the stack. One brother was on the stack; he'd put the hay where he wanted it.

As a little kid, I just loved horses. I was told not to go into the barn . . . I think I was round about two years old. Our barn was a ramshackle kind of thing; it was really too low. There was a window, long and not very high in front of the horses, where they put the hay through. This is in the olden times, eighty-some years ago. . . .

I'd manage to get out of the house. I could lift up the boards that covered the window, and I'd crawl in. There was this white team. The mare was awful; she was finicky. I never bothered her, but I used to crawl in there and get a curry comb from the box that was above. The old horse's name was Fred; I'd curry his legs. He was gentle, but his mate wasn't. She'd snort and stamp. I never went over into her part. I got scolded a lot for [going into the barn], but I don't remember getting a spanking for it.

The first horse I ever owned was a young pinto that was running in the hills around home. We knew who he belonged to. I wrote and told them I had him, and I bought him. His name was Buddy. I paid fifteen dollars, which was a lot of money for me then. I was, oh, up in my teens.

At home we were supposed to clean out the stall of the horse we used. That way the barn didn't get so dirty. We bedded them down in straw if they stayed in the barn overnight. We fed them. I think it's true all over; it's the girls that really like the horses.

I finished [breaking Buddy myself]. I don't know if he ever really got [broke]. He used to make my shoulder so sore. I'd try to get on him; he'd let me get my foot in the stirrup and make a grab for the saddle horn. Then he'd jump. We used to go round and round. He was a booger. I think pintos are noted for that.

My oldest brother had a horse that I loved. She would run like nobody's business. I begged him to sell her to me, but he never would. I never did get her, but Suze and I were very good friends. I just loved her.

When you buy a horse, you look for . . . well, disposition. There's all kinds. And you want to know, do they have good legs under them. It depends on what you're going to use the horse for, too. A workhorse, he'd have to be sturdy; a riding horse, an easy gait, a compatible disposition. You can develop a bad disposition in any animal, but I think the good points are passed on.

I don't know why I love horses. I was born that way. You feel so good when you're on them. Oh, the smell of leather, new leather. That's perfume almost.

Horses are *very smart*. Betty [Eva's daughter] had this mare we bought. She was two or three years old; she'd been broken already. But that horse, she'd outthink you every chance she got. She opened barn doors and gates, and when she didn't want to go someplace, she'd rear up, turn her head around, and go the other way. The kids used to crawl all over her. Diana was kind of slow, didn't have too much pep. They rode her to school and like that.

As with most families of the time, Eva's family grew and gathered their own food as much as possible.

My mother was a wonderful gardener, and she had a nice garden spot. It had been a bedding place for sheep, and it really did work out fine. We raised practically everything we ate. When they first came, they set out apple trees. And there were some plum trees, nice big red and blue ones. People said we were crazy; those things wouldn't grow in this country. But they did. At that time, in the summer and in the fall, there was lots of service-berries and chokecherries, wild currants and gooseber-ries. There weren't any wild raspberries. You went up in the Crazy Mountains and found raspberries there.

The whole gang of us [picked berries]. Mom didn't go so much, but us kids, we'd have a washtub between two of us, carrying it when we started out, and each one would have a pail of some sort to pick in. We'd pick service-berries and chokecherries. They were delicious. There was a lot of them eaten, but we weren't scolded for that.

Mother canned fruit, made jelly and jam. We were always disappointed with the serviceberries. Fresh, they were delicious; serviceberries and cream and sugar was something. But when she canned them, they seemed to lose their flavor. But we ate them. It was fruit. She also made chokecherry syrup to use on hotcakes.

We always had fruit and vegetables, and of course we always had chickens. We raised our own potatoes and carrots. They packed carrots in sand in the root cellar. They lasted quite a while. She canned peas and beans, made sauerkraut.

[Making sauerkraut], that was quite a deal. We had—it must have been a thirty-gallon barrel. Of course it was very clean on the inside. We put the cabbage in it. My dad had made her a cutter. The frame was made from cedar wood, and he'd taken a file and made a blade to fix in it. And that's what we cut it on. We'd cut a while, then we'd put salt on, then stamp it, pound it. When they got it up—not clear to the top—they had a lid that fit down in there, and they would put weights on the lid. And that barrel was put behind the cookstove to keep warm. As it worked, the whole house smelled like sauerkraut. But we didn't mind too much. After it got all the working done—it would be several weeks—it was taken out and put in the root cellar. Later, if it didn't act like it was going to keep, Mother would put it in jars and process it, put it on the shelves.

Cabbages were hung from the ceiling by their roots, and they lasted quite a while. We had bins of rutabagas and turnips and potatoes. We used to raise something that was a cross between a sugar beet and a turnip, I suppose. It wasn't as sweet as a sugar beet. We didn't eat them very often. In the wintertime, every afternoon, someone had to go to the root cellar and cut them up in smaller pieces to be fed to the milk cows. The milk always tasted good, but I have wondered if it did make the milk taste different.

It was when the cows would eat too many dandelions, or this stuff we called "arnicky." It's got a yellow flower, and it's sticky. Sometimes the cows ate it, and I remember the milk didn't taste good then.

Meat was really a problem. We had chickens, and in the summertime we had hogs, but all we had was salt pork, ham, or bacon. That's all we could keep. There came a time when we had to can that even. In the fall, we didn't get much beef to eat because they had to sell it to live on. A little later we had more milk, and the butter and eggs paid for the groceries. Every week [butter and eggs] had to be taken to town [Livingston].

My dad would go to town, and very rarely, my mother would go. The older boys or older girls would go with him sometimes. I didn't get to go very much, being nearly the youngest.

Dad brought supplies from town, and then along towards fall, they would buy things [to put in] the two root cellars. Canned goods, you didn't have much at that time . . . tomatoes and different fruits. I remember the first can of pineapples we had. I got just a taste of it. Pass it around to eleven people, there wasn't much to divide up. I can't remember until later years of ever having another can of pineapple. Delicious!

We used to eat dandelion greens in the spring, cooked and raw. The raw ones we put a dressing on. [Dandelions] gave us some of the things we needed.

We never lacked for food, but I know there were times when it was pretty hard sledding. I can remember one Christmas, my dad had paid some of my uncle's debts, and it kind of depleted the money. Christmas came, and there wasn't anything to buy presents with. One of my older sisters made all kinds of clothes for the little doll I had. There was some Christmas hard candy, and that was it.

Another difficult time for the family was when Eva's brother, Harvey, was reported missing in action in World War I.

My older brother was over in France, and along in the fall we got a notice that he was missing in action. We never got anything more. Mom kept writing, we all kept writing, but we didn't get anything back.

We never heard anything from Harvey from October to May. There was a card came that he was going to be released, and finally, he just showed up. He had been wounded, shot in the arm [while] he was out on one of those lookouts. He wandered around, trying to find his company, but most of that company was annihilated. Some French people took him in, and that's when he got the flu. He just about died. That was a pretty hard winter, not to know what happened, whether he was dead or alive. All that and the flu [at home].

My next older brother got the flu. Oh, was he sick! He was out of his head about half the time. I remember when they took him out of the house, wrapped in coats to keep him warm, put him in the car, and took him to an aunt's at Clyde Park. The doctor thought he needed to be kept warmer than he was upstairs at our house. It took Ed a long time to get well. He made it through—he had pneumonia, too—but it was nip and tuck.

Later, along toward spring, is when the rest of us got the flu so bad. They closed our school because of it. At that time, the neighbors were having it, too. There was an old couple down on Fall Crick who were sick. My sisters next older than I took turns riding every day to check on them.

The flu would be pretty bad for at least a week. You felt terrible, so achy and awful, just all in. And then you wouldn't feel very good for another week or so.

We didn't have much for treatment. They were kept warm, poultices on the chest. I'll tell you a remedy my mother used: sage tea. She'd have us pick the tenderest stems on the sagebrush and the leaves when they were green. I don't know how she ever got onto that [recipe]. If we got a fever . . . to get somebody to drink it, that was something else. It tasted terrible! But it worked, it worked.

Doctors then didn't want [patients] to eat heavy meals, meat and things like that, when they had the flu. There must have been some sense to it, because there was one young man who had the flu, and he'd gotten better. He wanted a steak. They gave him a steak, and he died. They said that was what caused it.

In the sparsely populated West, water was always a precious commodity. Water barrels were popular for storing water, but it was not always fit to drink.

After we got up in the other house—it was built ell-shaped—we had a barrel under [the eaves]. You never could drink that water. It was terrible-tasting, off the shingles, I guess. I tell you, we packed water. We even packed water to grow flowers in the yard. My mother was great for flowers. She always had geraniums in the house. Every Saturday, it was my job to get the wash-tub out and set them in there and sprinkle them, wash them. I still have geraniums.

We had sweet williams, dianthus, and later, irises. When they came out here, they brought a bunch of rosebushes from their home back in Iowa. We had those along the yard fence.

We always had the water pail with the dipper in it in the house. Everybody drank from the dipper; it's a wonder we lived.

When we were under the hill [in the homestead cabin], we walked just a little ways to water. We had a nice spring that came out of a bank there. We never had running water in the house, of course, but Dad had fixed it so we could put a pail under a spout [in the bank] and have running water.

They built a little springhouse off to the side. There wasn't water running through it, but it was cool in there, and that's where we used to put the milk and butter. We called it a milk house. They kept eggs in the root cellar. And it wasn't very far from the house.

When we moved to the larger house, we continued to get water from the spring, but we had to carry it uphill, which we did for many years. It took a good many buckets every day for our large family, especially on wash day. It was a scrub board deal. Later we got a washing machine. You stood there and went like this, and the thing inside—the agitator—went like that. Then, after I was married, and the two girls next older than I weren't at home, my brothers got my mother a Maytag washing machine with a gas engine. That's what happens when *men* have to do the work!

Heavens! It must have taken ten, twelve, fifteen trips. With two pails. We had one of those big wash boilers. We heated the water in that, boiled the white clothes. Used part of [the water] in the tub with a washboard. [A second tub was used for rinsing.] Later, we got this thing that had two tubs with a wringer in the middle. You turned the wringer by hand. It was heaven! You didn't have to squeeze all those old sheets and men's long john underwear and overalls. I hated that.

In the wintertime, clothes were usually hung outside. We'd bring them in, and some of them would have to be thawed out. Mom had a clothes rack that folded up, with rods you could hang things over. Quite often she put the rack in the living room.

We had a big Round Oak heating stove. It had a rail clear around the bottom where you could put your feet up and keep them warm. It heated the living room and the [downstairs] bedroom. The dining room got part of it, and some [heat] came into the kitchen.

In later years, they put a vent over the heating stove that went to the upstairs bedrooms. That was a lot nicer, but when you went to bed in the cold night, you took your rock or your flat iron, pulled the covers up over your head.

Up in the new house, we had a big kitchen wood-stove with a warming oven up above. You could put food up there, and it would stay warm. And then an old kitchen cabinet that was metal on top. You pulled out a board; that was your board for rolling pies and so forth. Below, there was a flour bin and a sugar bin and a couple of drawers for knives and such. In the dining room we had another [cabinet]. We put food in the bottom of it, and the top had dishes and the knife-and-fork drawers. Mom's cabinet was different from what most of the other women had. She didn't have a sink. [She washed dishes] on the stove, the back end of the stove. The rinse pan would be on the reservoir that we put water in and the stove heated. That's how we washed dishes. I didn't mind washing dishes, but I hated drying them. Still do. Kind of.

In her matter-of-fact way, Eva recounted meeting her future husband, Warren.

Met him at a dance. He came around and asked me to dance. I didn't know him; I danced with him and couldn't get rid of him. I got married when I was twenty-one.

We didn't have a wedding. Just went and got married. We were married in the parsonage. We went to Yellowstone Park [on our honeymoon] and on down to Salt Lake, and we ended up at the Grand Canyon. We saw Zion, we came back by Bryce, stayed there a day or two. Back to Salt Lake where we saw *Rose Marie,* the operetta.

And would you believe it, on a hundred bucks! We camped, you see. We carried our camping stuff in the back of the car.

After Warren and I got back from our honeymoon, we were given a shivaree. We were in bed, and all of a sudden there was this awful racket. Gramp came to the stair door. "Warren," he says, "get up! All hell's broke loose!" It was my own brothers and sisters, mostly. They came in, and we had something to eat. There wasn't any big ruckus about it.

We started housekeeping in a sheep wagon, lived in it for several months, 'til we got our house fixed so we could live in it.

You know what a wagon bed looks like. The sides were built up, and the middle [of the wagon], that's where you walked. At the back end was the bed; a hinged table came down [from above]. You had to make the bed before you could have breakfast. And the stove! It was a little old [wood-burning] stove that had an oven in it. I tried making a pie. The bottom didn't bake. It was terrible.

There was some cupboard space, but not very much. We had just enough dishes for two. That was it. Clothes were in suitcases down underneath where we kept the flour and sugar. There was no place to hang them.

Under the bunk, where we stored things, we had some sugar, also honey. Warren had found a bee tree, and I had got the honey. One night, all of a sudden, the sheep wagon started rockin'. We didn't know what was the matter. There were dogs sleepin' under [the wagon], and they were raisin' Cain. Warren got up. He said it was a bear. He shot off his gun, and it ran off. That was my first experience with a bear.

We didn't live in [the sheep wagon] through a winter, [although] I imagine we could have kept as warm in there as we did in that house. He'd put on siding, but he should have put some building paper underneath to keep the wind out. The wind came in. That was a cold house, I tell you. There were just three rooms: the living room where we ate, the kitchen, and bedroom.

The kitchen wasn't very wide. Cupboards over here, the stove over there, and the wood box. Very crude. We didn't [have running water]. [Eventually], there was a well with a pump on the back porch.

The DePuys lived for about four years in the little house that Warren built. During that time, two children were born.

Betty's the oldest, she was born in '27, David in '28, thirteen months later. I tell you, I was a tired woman that first year of David's life. Washing, a continuous washing. Two in diapers for a while. Washed on a scrub board in the kitchen, boiled the clothes in wash boilers. Heated the water in them, too. I didn't have a wringer. Just wrung them out, man force. It is hard. Sheets and overalls and stuff like that. Maybe it was good for our wrists, I don't know. In the wintertime, the house would get steamy.

[On wash day] we would pump enough water so we could fill one of those wash boilers that we'd put on the stove. That's the way we started out. We used part of that water in the washtub to wash with. The rest of it we left in the boiler to boil the clothes, the white clothes.

A long time later we got one of those [washers] with a tub on each end and a wringer in the middle. Eventually, we got a Sears washing machine with a gas engine. The tub was of material like a washboard. The seam around the bottom got to leaking from the vibration. We'd get it soldered up, and it'd be all right for a week or so, but then, well, we got through it. It worked a lot better than washing clothes on the washboard.

The DePuy family moved from the little house that Warren built to a larger preexisting dwelling on the ranch.

We thought it was more convenient than what we'd had, but it was kind of a cold house. When those old north blizzards used to come in there, it was hard keeping the kids warm, but we survived.

There were three bedrooms, a living room, a big kitchen where we ate, and there was a pantry. [In the wintertime] we'd get up in the morning, and the teakettle was frozen on the stove. It took a little while to get things thawed out.

To start with, we carried water from the crick. There was a well, but we didn't know whether we should use it. We didn't know what shape it was in. We were afraid some animal might have got in there. They opened it up, and it was fine. Warren bought a sink [that] we used to wash in. The water pail was beside it, right inside the kitchen door.

Warren would get enough wood for me to cook breakfast and to start dinner, but from then on, it was up to me. I wouldn't have minded chopping wood or getting dinner, if I could have done just one. But they didn't work so good together. We used coal whenever we had it, which wasn't too often. It holds heat so much better than wood.

I can't say that I was a very good cook, but we survived. I can think of a lot of other things I'd rather do. You didn't mind so much [cooking for hired help] until they started complaining, and then you felt like taking a frying pan to their heads. One guy got canned for [complaining].

There was always ashes on the top of the oven. I'd have to rake that off, and then I'd have to open the thing underneath the oven. You didn't have to do this every day, just once in a while. Scrape all the soot and stuff out so the air can circulate, and then you had to take the ashes out of the front of it. It flew all over the house sometimes, depending whether there was a breeze. We rarely got along without one.

I put the ashes on my garden. That's what my mother did. She put them around the apple trees, too. In the spring, they'd dig it in.

[During the cold months] we lived just in the kitchen part. The children would have to play in there because the rest of the house was so cold. In the morning, after they'd had their breakfast, they'd sit in a rocking chair. I'd put a blanket or a quilt over it and set them in there, side by side, put it right in front of the oven and I'd open the oven door. That helped.

There were always hot water bottles . . . a hot water bottle at their feet at night. It would have been a blessing to have had the kind of nightclothes they have now with feet in them and all that. That would have been wonderful.

Ever' time a blizzard came up there was danger. I remember one time, it was kind of melting; it was warm that morning. Warren decided to go over to the fur farm in Dillon for something. He left with the car, and I wasn't supposed to send the kids to school. But they wanted to go, so we saddled up the horse and they started off to school. The horse had more sense than we did, because she didn't want to go. They got to school all right, but then, right after the noon hour, that storm hit. Oh boy, it was terrible. I was about crazy. I didn't know what to do. The neighbors that lived close to the school took the kids in. One of the hired men and I made the trip over to the school in his truck. The teacher lived there at the schoolhouse, and she said they had gone down to the Ashers. We decided they were warm and being fed, so we came on home.

Oh dear, I don't know how late it was when Warren got home. [Before he left Dillon], he bought a lantern. He put the lantern down at his feet—cars didn't have heaters then—and he had a blanket that he covered himself with. He drove home, I don't know, two or three o'clock in the morning when he got there.

The hired man had brought in a whole pile of wood for me, and I had a fire going in that big old heating stove. I brought some blankets out of the bedroom, I pulled the davenport closer to the stove, and that's where I was sleeping. Oh dear . . .

Making a living in rural Montana was not for the faint of heart.

When we were first married, Warren's folks had sheep, and then that Depression came and they sold the sheep. Had a few cattle, not very many. Warren got started raising mink and foxes. Guess what job I got? Feeding the things. Packing out pail after pail of feed and dishing it out to them. That was quite a job.

We had a good business going until, well, Warren always blamed that English prince that was supposed to inherit the throne—Edward. They didn't have their coronation as they had hoped. And it knocked the mink market into the ditch. That was a blow. Warren decided to pelt off all the mink, but he kept the foxes. And the next year you couldn't sell a long-furred pelt. They didn't bring enough to pay for the feed. They had gone out of style. That put an end to the fur business.

Then they started in cattle. They got some purebred Herefords and such. That went on for a good many years. We still have cattle. They got the idea of starting a fish hatchery. We built a big building, put in tanks. It was a profitable business until the highway came through and went over the top of it. Of course, we got paid for it, but all that work!

Warren had always wanted some white swans. After we got the white ones, he saw these black ones advertised, so we bought a pair of those. At the same time,

I bought some peacock eggs and hatched five; four of them lived. Those have all died, but I do have a pair down here that the Osens gave me for my birthday a couple of years ago. They fly, you know, and they're like a turkey, they nest on the ground. I raised one litter. She had her nest out there by the chicken house. The next year she hatched some, but the old hoot owl got all of them. I thought, I'll put eggs in a pen and cover it, keep them in there until she's hatched her babies. They fly awful young, those little peacocks. She laid four eggs in the dead of winter this year. [The eggs] got really chilled; I don't think they'll hatch. Later she laid three more. I don't know, I don't think I'll get any little peacocks this year.

The males are beautiful, but I think the females are cute. They go around so quiet and reserved, like they're trying to tell you that all peacocks aren't like those old males.

Cattle, sheep, a fur farm, and a fish hatchery . . . long hours and hard work. But looking back over her many years, Eva summed it up: "It's a good old life, if you can stand it." She was interviewed at her home in Livingston in April 1988. She died there at age ninety-three in June 1998.

FLORENCE LEWIS LYALL

*"Baking in a woodstove is a
guess-and-by-golly thing."*

Florence Lyall was born on June 10, 1902, near Emigrant, Montana. She was a sweet but spunky woman, and a hard worker. She had lovely pale red-gold hair. She could still remember the house she had been born in—a small, one-story log house with a shingle roof. There was only one bedroom, but as was often found in those days, there was a bed in the living room.

The house was built kind of on a hillside, and there were three steps down to the kitchen from what we called the front room. There was a big, long bench right on that same wall where the cookstove was. The table sat out in the middle of the floor. And cupboards, not too many of them.

We had water in the house, piped in from Davis Crick in the canyon up above. That was very unusual in 1900.

Then in 1910, my father built a new house. It was a nice home, quite a transition. It had four bedrooms upstairs, all hardwood floors downstairs. Beautiful old doors, doors that you don't see anymore. There was a nice-sized dining room where we always ate. Off the dining room was a bedroom and big bathroom with hot and cold water.

There was a swing door between the kitchen and the dining room, a large closet in the kitchen and a large pantry. Along the south side of the house, there was a nice porch. A front porch, too, overlooking the mountains.

We had no centralized heating in those days. There was a wood-and-coal range in the kitchen; in the dining room we had one of those big heaters that used coal. About three years after the house was built, we had gaslights put in. Gas was piped in some way. The gaslights were all downstairs because they were a fire hazard.

We always ate in the dining room, the hired help, too. Nothing fancy, but that was where we ate. The hired help were treated like family. All of them lived on the ranch; my mother even washed for them. Can you believe that? Eight, ten men around there, and she had all their beds to keep up.

I get rather disgusted with some of the young women nowadays. They complain so. Even I had it easy, and I didn't have the conveniences that I have now. I mean . . . grief! My mother had to do *everything* the hard way.

Baking day was just about every day. Although she didn't bake bread every day, she did a lot of baking of cookies and cakes. She always set a good table with some kind of dessert. Pies or puddings, that sort of thing.

Father did chores before breakfast. Breakfast was served, I s'pose, around 6:30, because he had to be out in that field the minute he could get organized to get there. Breakfast was hotcakes, biscuits, or waffles, and my dad always wanted potatoes. They were cooked the night before, then hash-browned. There was plenty of jam on the table. And cereal, usually cooked cereal. Some prepared cereals, corn flakes, and Sunny Jim. As a kid, I thought it was super. But cereal was mostly oatmeal, not much fruit. If we had fruit, it was at noon or evening.

The noon meal was always meat and potatoes, some kind of vegetable, and dessert. Always bread, of course. And the evening meal, which we called supper, was the same. They were all hearty meals. They had to be. The men expected it, and they needed it, too. And a big bowl of fruit on the table. Canned fruit. We used a lot of dried fruit in those years, too. One of the things my mother used to serve was dried apples and dried raspberries cooked together.

There used to be a man who traveled through the neighborhood once or twice a year. My dad would order prunes, twenty-five pounds of them, twenty-five pounds of dried apples. Peaches, too. Coffee. All that sort of stuff, he'd order from him. Then it would be shipped by train to Emigrant. He'd go over and pick it up. All that stuff was kept in the pantry.

Our meat was mainly pork. We'd kill eight hogs, and they were all smoked. The meat was put in a brine in a big, big barrel. The brine was salt and brown sugar and something else. It had to float an egg. That brine had to be strong enough to hold the egg up. The meat was kept in the brine for a while, then taken out and put in the smokehouse. My dad was very particular about the smokehouse. He took care of the hams and the shoulders and the bacon, all that. We had to eat the ribs in a hurry. It didn't take long. We had others around.

The meat stayed in the brine about six weeks. In the smokehouse, you let it dry out, then my dad liked to use apple branches to smoke with for a special flavor. The meat hung down from the ceiling, tied with twine, binding twine. Dad did all that himself, and nothing was ever done in the smokehouse except the smoking of meat. It was a pretty good-sized building. I have an idea it took several weeks, but I couldn't say for sure. After the meat had been smoked, I think he kept it hanging in the smokehouse. As I remember, that's where we went to get it. There was a door, no windows, no danger of flies or anything like that.

Memories of her father's smokehouse triggered the recollection of an incident that happened many years later.

My husband's brother, Oscar, was quite a guy. An industrious type, didn't know anything but work, that's the truth. He lived on the other side of the ranch. He'd come up, and they'd work together. He always ate the noon meal here. I had this big ham that I'd cooked up and thought it was properly taken care of. I put the whole thing on the table, cut down into it, and oh dear, here was [whispers] a whole bunch of maggots! My husband just had a *fit!* "Oh," says Oscar, "cover it up with mustard, you'll never know the difference."

Florence's recollections of her early childhood were of simple pleasures on the ranch.

As I remember my childhood, I was outside most of the time. I loved to tag along after my dad. My sister was four years younger than I. She was a chubby little fat one, couldn't walk very fast. That kind of annoyed me. In the first place, I didn't want her taggin' after me.

When I'd see my dad out in the field, I'd take out after him. I liked to be with him, kind of a special thing.

We had a little irrigating ditch that I had to jump over. I could get over easy, but my sister was little, short-legged, not too agile anyway. One time I saw Dad out in the field, and here she came. She didn't get across that little ditch; she fell in it, on her back. My father's uncle, my great-uncle, who often stayed with us, happened to see her, and it's a good thing he did. She would have drowned, no doubt about it.

Boy, did he paddle me! And I had every bit of it coming. You see, she was stuck there; the water was backing up on her. I can laugh now, because it was kind of funny when you stop and think how she wedged that ditch shut. This was such a deep little ditch; it wasn't any wider than . . . a shovel ditch is what it was. Kids! They don't think of the consequences, ever.

The spring of the year, we couldn't wait to get up the road, which was back of the house, to look for buttercups. Thrilled to death when we found some. My mother kept her eyes on us, but we were wandering around, here and there.

We played Flinch and Lotto; we played dolls; we had tea parties. She was Mrs. White, I was Mrs. Black. We were always playing Going to Missouri; Mother came from Missouri. Once we went out to the chicken house, and we sat down on the roosts and got lice! Chicken lice on our heads! It was about noon, and here we came to the house, both of us crying and having fits. Poor Mother, she was in the middle of getting the last-minute things ready for the noon meal.

I can still remember, she dipped my head in the ditch. She got rid of the lice in the cold water of the ditch. She didn't know what else to do, poor thing.

We went into town—Livingston—only twice a year. We got provisions over here in Emigrant. My dad did all the buying. Not because he didn't feel my mother wasn't capable; it was just more convenient for him to go. He hauled hay over there for Yellowstone Park, two trips a day, three or four wagons per trip. If anything was needed, she'd make a list. He'd pick it up and bring it back.

There used to be a dentist at Emigrant. First and only time I had ever been near a dentist, my dad took me there. I had a toothache. You should have seen that office. Cluttery! Instruments here . . . dust . . . cluttered up. But he pulled the tooth, and I got rid of the toothache.

In the spring, my mother and sister and I went down to Livingston on the train. This was more for clothing and that sort of thing. But in the fall, when the fair was on—my father liked fairs—the whole family went. We'd stay in town for about three days. That was quite a thing, you know. We had no electricity, and to see electric lights was just something special.

Later, Florence's parents passed away, and she was sent to attend the Annie Wright Seminary in Washington State for several years. She returned to Livingston for her senior year of high school. In December 1920, she and Ralph Lyall were married.

I was eighteen and not quite a half when I married Ralph. We were married in the courthouse in Big Timber [Sweet Grass County, Montana]. I had my own car. Of course, he had a car, but we used mine. There was another couple that went with us. We were married by the justice of the peace. It was not an elopement, because we were on our own. We spent our honeymoon in the Northern Hotel in Billings. At that time it was lovely. That was back in 1920.

We lived about eight miles south of Livingston on the Mortimer ranch. That's who owned it when the Lyalls bought it in 1915. It was an old log house, one of the oldest in the valley. We did a lot of work on it. When I went there as a bride, nothing had been done to it. The place had been rented, off and on for years, before the Lyalls bought it; then Ralph and his brothers batched there. You should have seen that house! You can't imagine the shape it was in. The room off the kitchen that was eventually turned into a bedroom was filled with wheat. Mice? You bet your life! I was never afraid of mice until I went there.

We had a pantry off the kitchen. This little room was dark, dark, dark. And it was the only place I could put pots and pans. In those days in log houses, they put sheeting material on the ceiling, on the walls, too. Well, I'd go in there to get a pot or a pan, and a darn mouse'd run over my hand. Imagine the lack of sanitation. They got it cleaned up for me, put a window in the end, painted up, sealed in, so forth and so on.

And the old stove I started keeping house with . . . you put the wood in through a little door. We used some coal, too. It had a reservoir at one time, but when I fell heir to it, there was no reservoir; you had to prop up the oven door when you baked.

We were married the first part of December, and the first winter Ralph's mother would send down half-gallon jars of fruit and pickles, big round loaves of bread. She churned butter and sent that down. No longer having a mother of my own, she really took me under her wing.

Finally, I said, "Mother, I've got to learn to do this. You have no business doing it for me. It's my problem." So she showed me how.

[To make bread] you'd have yeast cakes, yeast foam they called it, or magic yeast. Little squares, and oh, were they hard. You cooked potatoes at noon, boiled them, always. You saved the potato water and a few potatoes to mash in with it. They had to be mashed up pretty fine or you'd have chunks in the bread. Let that cool down, then put the yeast cake in. Usually one did it, nicely. That evening you stirred the flour into it, some salt, and maybe a little sugar to make what you call a sponge. I had a big two-gallon crock that I put it in. I'd set it in a pan of warm water, put it on the back of the stove during the night. Of course, the water got cold.

In one of my first experiences, the sponge hadn't raised up like I thought it should. It had gotten really chilled, so I set it on the back of the stove. I didn't have much space there, and I cooked the bottom of the sponge. Well, you know what that did to it, it killed it completely. It had to be thrown out, and in those days that wasn't very good.

Finally I learned to do it right. Got so I liked to do it. It was just one of those things you learned to do.

Baking in a woodstove is a guess-and-by-golly thing, but you learn, you learn. I found just by watching when to put my cakes in the oven. I'd open the oven a little bit to see if everything was okay, if they were raising or hadn't fallen or something else. . . .

Knowing how hot to build the fire, that was another thing. You kind of watched that. I didn't like to bake with coal. I never did get so I knew what I was doing with it. The wood, I could put in so many sticks, and when it got to about the point where I thought it was okay, I would put my food in the oven. I burned stuff. I burned up some cakes one time when I was having a group in. I had to throw [them] out. Oh, I hate to do that, but if you get your fire too hot, it can happen. You had to learn to gauge your fire.

It took about half an hour for your woodstove to heat up. I had one with two lids in front, and then the rest of it was a big flat metal area. That was real nice, just slide things back.

Some people used to take the lid off and set the pot down over the open fire. Never I. I didn't like black-bottomed pots at all. No, you try to get a good fire going, and then you put the pots on the two front lids. Or slide 'em back to the side. They cooked fast enough.

The damper controls your heat. Turn it down, but don't turn it down too far, or you'll have smoke in the house. If you've got a good chimney and it draws too well, you're letting everything go up the chimney. As you use the damper, you learn how far to turn it.

In the wintertime, I always made a batch of oatmeal or some kind of cereal I could put in a double boiler. It tastes differently, too. It's a more finished taste. Nowadays I use Quaker's one-minute cereal, no time at all, but it doesn't taste like the oatmeal you put in the double boiler and left all night long.

They used to have a stove polish—blackening—and I did use it for a while. I'd get real industrious 'n' polish. Oh, they look lovely when you first polish them, but start wiping off, and all you've got is black on everything you touch. I got so I scrubbed it up good, and for the top part I used paraffin, not a lot, just enough to give a good shine. That was on the part that would be heated. The rest was scrubbed by hand. Years ago they used to use sand for polishing. I never did. I didn't like the mess of it. Most of the time I just scrubbed it with soap and water.

In my kitchen, and mine was pretty much like all the rest, I had a cabinet where I rolled out my cookies and worked my bread and kept my dishes up above. No water in the house 'til we'd been married five years. I hated baking day before I got water in the house. You didn't have a place to put things to soak. Everything dried up. When I got my first Chore Boys, all I had to do was scrub a little bit. I thought it was a lark!

When we got water in the house, my goodness, what a difference it made in the work. I had three little kiddies to bathe every morning, and washing every day. You washed every day, and that was done by hand. The men had always carried water up, all kinds of water, but when you're giving baths and washing, you run out. It takes an awful lot. There were always dishes to wash, that sort of thing. But it didn't hurt me.

Once I had a fire in the living room heater. There was an elbow that went back in where the heater pipe went up the chimney. It wasn't insulated well at all. I had started the fire in the heater so it would start getting the room warm. I went back to check, and my gosh, the room was full of smoke! Gives you a thrill, I'll tell you.

I started looking, and I could see a flame up there. It was a short chimney, so what do I do—I hated the mess—I got water real quick and threw it on and put it out. You watched for chimney fires pretty carefully, especially in an old house. You knew the chances of a fire if you didn't. No fire department, absolutely not.

Oh, that living room! Part of the floor was cut out. We got that fixed, then we papered. After we papered, I brought my piano down. We had worked so hard, cleaning and getting the front room all fixed up. It looked real nice. Later, when I moved the piano to clean behind it, there wasn't any wallpaper on the wall. The mice had eaten it all up! We had used flour paste, that's the reason. I was so disgusted.

We built on two porches, a porch on the kitchen door and one on what we called the front door. Just little old ordinary porches, but it was quite an improvement. Certainly beat having them step from outside directly into the house. You made improvements gradually. You didn't do it all at once, that's for sure.

When I was first married, I didn't have a washing machine, just a washboard. Eventually I got a Maytag washer that had a gasoline motor. My husband used to get awfully provoked with me. I'd crank and crank and crank on that darn thing. It'd heat up, it wouldn't work, but I would *not* go back to that washboard for anything! I think I worked harder than if I had gotten the washboard and used it. I had the Maytag until we got electricity on the ranch in '45.

In the summertime, how I hated ironing. The kitchen was so hot. You heated your irons on the stove, baked bread the same day. You're goin' great guns, noon meal to run up, ironing for four hours. You had to use every hour you had, that's the truth about it. And then as the kiddies came along, it was more so.

We had a diversified operation: Hereford cattle, seed peas, and grain. Our pea crop was quite important because it was a cash crop, the raising of seed peas that we got from D. M. Ferry. He used to be a prominent seed grower. Usually they turned out pretty good, and as I say, they were a cash crop which the farmer needed badly in the fall before the cattle were sold. Cattle weren't sold until the first of October or later. Then there was the grain, which was held over for a while. Just like they do nowadays.

Peas were very touchy. In those days it meant irrigating by hand. If you irrigated them at the wrong time, the blossoms would drop off, but if they were handled properly, they did very well. One year we had a patch near the house, seven acres, and it was hit by frost. It was the middle of June, and they were up and blooming. Our hired man said, "Cut 'em down. They'll never make anything." My husband said, "No, we'll leave them. At least we can use them for feed." You know, those things came out, bloomed again, made forty bushels to the acre.

Peas were mowed at a certain stage, just like hay, except you had a roller thing that rolled the peas back. Someone came along behind and mowed them off, and then they were put up in little shocks. That's the way they were gathered and put through the threshing outfit. It had to have a special sieve. Ferry furnished nice seamless sacks, so we didn't have to buy those.

The first year I was married, I had a lot to learn, what to buy, how to buy, and so on. We were married in December, another brother in February, one in June. Since they were all in partnership, they thought the best thing to do would be to charge the groceries to the partnership. I didn't go for it, but it seemed to be the thing to do.

Fall came, time to pay the grocery bill. It was five hundred dollars. Oh, they just went up in smoke! I got the brunt of it. I was young, on and on. I didn't know much about buying, blah, blah. One sister-in-law was a teacher and should have been well informed, but she was the extravagant one. You didn't buy shelled nuts in those days; you didn't buy a lot of things that she did. Fair is fair, and I didn't like being told that I hadn't held down my end of it. I got my dander up. I told Ralph and his brothers, "We're going to have milk cows. Other women around the valley pay their grocery bills with milk cows."

We got our milk cows, and they paid for our groceries, they paid for our gas, and even some contribution to the church. Usually we milked about six cows. And then it was hard to get help. Awfully hard to get help that wanted to do chores. You have milk cows, you have chores to do.

My husband's brother was going to go over and stay on the range that year. We had a lot of cattle over there, accessible to people who wanted to come in and help themselves. So we always had a herder. I knew my husband was worried, wondering about help. I said, "I don't know if I can do it, but I'll take on milking the six cows."

I took on the cows, and I had them the rest of my life. Of course, when there were extra men around, like my brother-in-law, then he did the milking. I got along just fine, but I told my husband, "If a cow ever kicks me, you'll never get me in that barn again." I was afraid of them.

We sold cream. It was usually sour, and then it was taken down to the creamery in Livingston. You got a pretty good price out of your cream. Butterfat content had a lot to do with it. It was a good income.

A cow, when she comes fresh, gives about three gallons, an ordinary milk pail, maybe a little bit more. The Holsteins were the ones that gave the milk. We weren't especially fond of them, but we did have some. When she came fresh, boy, she filled that pail like nothing in just one milking. So you could say six gallons a day is what a cow will give. I don't know how they rate that now.

Holsteins don't have rich milk. It's milk, but it's not rich milk like a Guernsey or Jersey. We had a neighbor; he'd call us up, want to know if we'd want a dairy calf. We could go and get it for the getting. For a fact, that's where we got most of our milk cows in later years. Not long ago someone told me they want forty or fifty dollars for them now. I guess we had some good times, too.

We didn't have a cream separator when we had only one milk cow for our own consumption. Put our milk in pans, and I skimmed off the cream. My husband loved that. The thicker the better. He liked it on cereal or anything.

We had bucket calves that we fed the skim milk to. If we had too much for the bucket calves, maybe we had a few pigs we could feed it to. There were a few times we had to throw it over the hill. About breaks your heart to do that. For the most part we were able to use it.

I stayed alone on the ranch when the men were over on the range. I'd be home alone almost a week. I remember one time, taking my husband to the range at Cokedale, we drove by our milk cows, and my husband said, "Now that cow there won't come fresh until . . . she'll be all right until I get back."

She was a Holstein with a terrible big bag on her, and she was ornery on top of it. I got back that evening about 5:30, and here was a little calf layin' out there. I had to get her into the barn, get the rest of them in, too. And she would kick! Oh, she was mean. I knew I had to put the hobbles on, but oh boy, was I scared. You learn to do these things. I wouldn't do it now. But anyway, I got the hobbles on her. Here she was, tryin' to kick those hobbles off. On either side of her, the milk cows were smaller. She was a great big old thing like those Holsteins are. Darned if she didn't go down and fall on top of another cow.

I didn't know what to do. Here I was alone; I tried to get her up. I hit her in the tail end. She wouldn't get up. I think she could hardly get up, to be honest about it. You know your cow barns, you kept them clean, but still they urinate and so forth and so on. They're slick. I got me a pitchfork and got in front of the manger. I didn't get too vicious. She finally got up, and I got her milked. Then the thing was to get the calves, the little bucket calves, to drink their milk. That's quite a process, I tell you.

I learned to be a good ranch wife, and we were as happy in those days as we ever were, I guess.

Florence Lyall was interviewed in her home near Chico Hot Springs in Paradise Valley, Montana, in March 1983. She died in Great Falls in 2002, three months shy of her one-hundredth birthday.

KAIA LIEN COSGRIFF

"It never came to us that we were poor."

Born in Norway on June 19, 1899, Kaia Lien Cosgriff was one of thousands of immigrants who came to Montana from Scandinavia as a young child. She was a tiny, independent woman who was especially proud of being named the "Centennial Queen" at the local rodeo when she was in her eighties. Eager to share her life stories, she was animated as she described her upbringing.

My brother, a younger sister, and I were all born in Norway. Everybody over there was very poor, and my father was having a hard time to provide for the family. When he had saved enough money, he came to the United States.

He tended sheep and worked on ranches; he worked for Arnesons on the Yellowstone River [near Springdale, Montana]. In 1904, when I was five, he sent for Mom and us three kids. My sister was born after he left.

I can remember leaving Norway. All of Mama's relatives and friends were there; everybody was crying and crying. I lay down on the ground and kicked; I didn't know what it was all about.

We were awfully seasick. We vomited almost all the time we were on that ship. We slept in tiers. There were windows clear up at the top. We opened the windows sometimes. I don't remember very much about the trip. I don't know how my mother ever managed Ellis Island with those three little kids. Or how she found a train to come to Springdale.

I should have asked Mother, but, I don't know, we just grew up and kind of forgot about those things. Now I wonder why I didn't ask about a lot of things. I'm the oldest one in the family. Some of my brothers and sisters know nothing of this history. Nothing! I was twenty-three when my youngest brother was born. When I tell them things, they're amazed.

We came from New York to Springdale, where my dad was working. When we got to Springdale, Dad was there to greet us, hugging us. My sister, born after our father left Norway, said, "Mama, isn't that a nice man?"

The first Christmas we were all together, Dad had to split wood all day. In Norway they celebrated from before Christmas until after the New Year, one big long celebration. It was terrible hard on them to have him split wood on Christmas Day and then work all the other days. They didn't know anyone, didn't have any celebration. Dad could talk a little bit of English, but

Mother couldn't. We lived there in W. D. McKenzie's bunkhouse—it must have been a year—then Dad went down the Yellowstone River and built a cabin out of cottonwood trees. It had a dirt floor and a dirt roof. In the summertime, weeds would grow on the roof.

There was one small room . . . one little bit of a room. Dad made a door and frames for two windows, one on either side of the cabin. He made two beds out of rough lumber; our mattresses were made of straw. There was a bed in this corner and a bed in that corner. The stove was here, and Mama had two apple boxes stacked in this corner. That was her cupboard. Dad made a table out of rough lumber, and that was under one window. We sat on boxes around the table.

All three of us, my brother, my sister, and I, slept in one bed. Mama and Dad slept over on the other side of the room.

Mama cooked on a tinny little stove like they used to have in camp wagons. It had a little oven and a stove-pipe that went through the roof.

They bought kerosene in five-gallon cans for the coal-oil lamps. When the can was empty, Dad would cut it, one side, then the other. He'd roll each side back to form a boiler. Mama heated water in it right on the stove. She always boiled the clothes. Everybody did in those days. In spring, summer, and fall, she washed the clothes on a washboard in the river and hung them on sagebrush to dry. "Oh," she said, "the sun makes the clothes so white and pretty." I can't remember how she dried them in the wintertime.

There was a spring at least a quarter of a mile from home. We carried water from the spring to cook and to drink. The rest of the water, we got it from the Yellowstone River. Mama had a bucket, and us kids had little buckets. It seems to me we went up to the spring every morning.

When my mother wanted to sweep the floor, she'd take an axe and go out and chop the sagebrush. It was real high. She'd sweep the floor with the sagebrush; that was her broom. The dirt floor was hard as cement.

That sod roof never leaked. It didn't. I don't remember that place ever leaking.

During the time the Liens lived in their little cabin by the river on the Arneson Ranch, they were treated to visits from two Norwegian bachelor brothers who had a little cabin about a mile from their place.

They'd come down and visit us. They had a garden, and one time when they came, they brought us a big kettle full of beautiful ripe tomatoes. Oh, they were so pretty. Mother took them out of the kettle and sent it home with them. After they left, she said, "I don't know what those things are; they could be poison. I'd better taste them before you kids eat them." She took a bite. It was sour. She said, "It's poison! It's poison!" And she threw them all out.

One time when Sam and I went up to see the brothers, they gave us some nice little beets. They'd washed them clean, and they sent them home with us.

Mama said, "We'll have these"—she didn't have any name for them—"for supper tonight." She put them on the table; we tried to eat them raw.

The next time we went up there, they said, "Did you like the beets?"

"No, we couldn't eat them, they were so hard."

"Well, you're supposed to cook 'em."

It seemed in Norway all the vegetables they had were peas and potatoes, rutabagas, carrots, and cabbage. That's all the vegetables Mama ever talked about or knew anything about.

Like people in Norway, my folks ate a lot of fish. They would get little buckets of pickled herrings. They didn't have to cook them; they ate them with potatoes and bread.

Whitefish came in the Yellowstone in great big schools. Dad would go down the river a ways and throw in a stick of dynamite. Mother would sit in the boat; he'd come down, and they'd get a boatful of whitefish with a net. They'd take 'em home and clean 'em and put the whitefish in a brine in a big wooden barrel. They kept a long time. As long as they lived, my folks were hungry for fish. And do you know, not any of us kids like fish.

When we lived in the cabin on the Yellowstone, we drank tea. Mother made bread; we had potatoes. They bought dried fruit, dried peaches, and apricots. And they were good. We [children] didn't like fish, so we didn't eat any. I can't remember having any meat. They lived on fish.

There was no way the folks could keep potatoes from freezing. They'd put them under their bed; they

froze under the bed. Did you ever smell frozen potatoes? Awful! Terrible!

Eventually, Anton Lien, Kaia's father, changed jobs and went
to work for the Briggs and Ellis Ranch. He was gone for a week
at a time, and his wife, Bertha, stayed alone with the three
children.

She played with us all the time. We thought of her as
being the same age we were. She was sweet, she laughed
a lot.

Dad would come home on Saturday night. They'd
visit, but then Mama read the Bible to us almost all day
Sunday. Her father was a Lutheran minister. She'd clean
us up; we'd sit on the boxes. We couldn't do anything
but sit there and listen. We hated Sundays.

The stories she read to us, the songs she sang to
us, they're still with me. When I go to church and the
minister gets up and preaches, that's what my mother
taught us.

They took a [Norwegian language] newspaper, *The
Decorah Posten*. It was a big paper, like the *Billings Gazette*.
My mother saved them until she had a great big pile. She
thought she would fix the cabin so it'd look nicer. She
took flour and water, cooked it, and made a paste. Then
she spread these newspapers all over the walls. One night
those newspapers started to move. It was a rattlesnake
between the walls and the newspaper. I can remember
Mother and Dad talking—it must have been a Saturday
night—wondering if they should get up and try to kill it

or just leave it. To this day, I don't remember what they did.

There were so many rattlesnakes along the river. My mother didn't kill 'em; she'd say, "Now kids, you'd better let the rattlesnakes have this territory and you move over there." I don't know how we escaped being bit by rattlesnakes, they were so thick.

During the time the Liens lived in the cabin on the Yellowstone, Kaia's mother had a baby, the first member of the family to be born in the United States.

My sister Jetty was born in that cabin. No doctor, no midwife, my dad delivered her. He told us, "It's a beautiful little girl." He told my mother, "It's a *beautiful* little girl!" He delivered a lot of the children himself. Our mother was a very healthy woman.

[At first] we didn't have any chickens, and we didn't have any milk. Dad told us about eggs over on the Briggs and Ellis Ranch, eggs in the barn, eggs all over. Mother said, "Why don't you try to buy a couple of hens up there?" The next Saturday when he came home, he had two chickens in a sack on his back. Of course, no chicken house, so they turned them loose in the cabin with the dirt floor. In the morning those chickens were sitting on the foot of their bed. They'd gone to roost! Later that day, Dad fixed a little box for them. Oh, we were so excited over those two chickens. Can you imagine three kids with two chickens? They started to lay . . . dividing two eggs with three kids! We got so excited over those eggs. Eventually Dad bought a milk cow. We drank the milk; my mother churned the cream. Mother did the milking, of course.

Later, Dad dug a well right close to the cabin. We had a rope and a bucket. You let the bucket go down and it filled, and then you have to pull it up. They had a cover on it so we wouldn't fall in. Finally, they put in a pump, and we'd stand up there and pump all day.

Dad bought a boat. He'd cross the Yellowstone in the boat, walk down to Big Timber to get groceries and stuff, and row back. Practically ever'body in Big Timber spoke Norwegian. There was J. F. Solberg; he was from Norway, and that's where Daddy bought all our clothes and shoes and everything. He never took us to town to see if the shoes would fit. He just looked at them. If they were too big, that was fine.

Later, Dad bought a team of horses and a buggy. We used to go to town once a year. Mom and Dad and Sophie, they would sit in the seat, Sam and I would sit in a little cubbyhole in the back with our feet hanging out. We were in seventh heaven. We waited for that trip a whole year.

My dad'd always buy candy when we went to town. Just seeing people walking up and down the street was a treat in itself. We had only my uncles who also came to Montana to work and the two bachelors I told you about [for occasional company].

The Liens did not own the land on which the cabin on the Yellowstone stood. Unable to fence property that wasn't his,

Mr. Lien came up with a creative plan when he needed to protect a few sheep from predators.

They put the sheep on an island in the middle of the Yellowstone so the coyotes couldn't get to them. They had to take the sheep over in the boat. Mama would sit there and hold the ewes, and Dad would row the boat. It worked all right with the ewes, but when they got the buck in there, he raised a commotion. He jumped into the Yellowstone. Dad jumped in after him; Mama had to row. They got him out and into the boat and finally got him over to the island.

Sam and Kaia, who were the two oldest children, were given the freedom in the summertime to wander out in the hills. One day when they were out in a pasture, they walked up to some horses. They were thrilled to find that the horses were tame enough to pet.

When we went home that night, I took the drawstrings out of my petticoat and tied them into a rope. Next day I said to Sam, "Now we can go out and get our horse." We went out in the hills, and we found the horses. This one horse was nice and tame. He came up to us, and we put the string around his neck and led him home. There wasn't a porch; there was just a board outside the door. We stood on the board, and we said, "Mama, come see what we've got."

And she said, "Well, what is that?"

"It's a horse, a saddle horse."

"What're you going to do with it?"

We said we were going to ride it.

"Take it back where you got it." That was the last of the episode.

A lot of Norwegians from the part of the country where Kaia's parents had lived came to Big Timber and Sweet Grass County. Three of Kaia's uncles, her mother's brothers, came over.

My oldest uncle, Oscar, came here two or three times. He'd work for a time; he'd send money to Norway. He'd go back over there for a while and then come back to the United States and work some more. Eventually he went back to Norway and got married.

When two of my uncles were going back to Norway, they came [to say goodbye]. They brought Mama a winter coat. It was a black coat; it had a braid in front and in back. She wore that coat for twenty years.

Mama's brothers wanted her to go back to Norway. Her father kept writing to her. He'd say he wanted her back home, he wanted her to come back so bad. I don't know how she ever stood it, I truly don't, and still be sane.

She used to sing all the time. She'd learned all those hymns by heart, and she had a beautiful voice. Even when we were grown up, she'd still sing, doing her housework.

Mama used to tell me about her father. He was an unusually nice man. He was a minister; he taught school, too. Every night, after they'd gone to bed, he'd come up and say prayers with them and read the Bible. Every night he would do that.

When he was in church, he'd invite people to come home to visit them. Grandmother was so tired and wanted nothing to do with it, and she'd get real provoked with him for socializing like that. She didn't, she never did write a letter to my mother. It was always her dad who wrote to her. I don't know if she could write, and she was so busy all the time. It was always her father who wrote to all of his kids when they were gone. I wish I had one of those letters. I've never seen such beautiful handwriting.

My father never heard from any of his relatives. Never. In his whole lifetime. That was the way he wanted it. It was such an unhappy childhood.

His mother died when he was little, and there were quite a few children. His father married again, and there were more. The stepmother was partial to hers. He was out on his own when he was young. He worked on a boat; he constructed roads in Norway.

Anton Lien realized he would have to enroll the children in a school. He took a job in Melville, Montana, working for Teddy Lavold, feeding cattle and sheep, doing ranch work, and putting up hay.

We had a nice house to live in, four or five rooms, a mansion! We were thrilled. It was beautiful country, and we had kids to play with. Mother had nice neighbors that were good to her. They were Norwegian, so she could talk Norwegian to them.

I was going on nine when we went to the Basin Crick School, out in the country. We worshipped Mrs.

Lowry, our teacher. She was beautiful, and she was so good to us.

All those kids in the school were Norwegian, but they all talked English except us. Mrs. Lowry taught us English and had them interpret for her. When she gave us our first report cards, she told the other kids to explain to us: Take them home, show them to your parents, have the parents sign them, bring them back.

Learning English wasn't too hard. I remember her getting bottles and pencils, erasers and tablets and ink-wells. She'd say, "Kaia and Sam, come up here. What's this, what's that?" She was very, very kind. I don't think I've ever loved a teacher as much as I loved her.

When Dad worked for Teddy Lavold, he came home every night. We weren't too happy about that, because when we were naughty, Mother would say, "Just wait 'til your dad comes home." We had to think about it, and wait and wait. You know, that's no good. I made up my mind when I was real little, if I ever had any kids, if they needed a spanking, I wasn't going to wait 'til their dad came. They're going to get it right now.

After less than two years on the Lavold ranch, Anton Lien took up a homestead—160 acres—on Swan Creek.

When Dad took up that homestead over on Swan Crick, he built a cabin out of rough lumber. It had the door here, with a partition that divided the cabin in two rooms. Rough lumber on the inside, rough lumber for the floor, tar paper on the outside. In the wintertime, the room that had the beds got really cold. They cut part of the wall out so some of the heat from the cookstove would go into the other room.

We had to carry water uphill from a spring, but it was good water. We could use it for everything. We had a cow, so we had milk.

There was another family over in the next gulch. He was a carpenter, and he had built a nice little house. Dad decided they had money to fix a decent house. John Mathewson, the carpenter, came over and tore down the old tar-papered shack. They put the stove in the barn. There was just room for the stove and the beds. We called it a bunkhouse.

Vesta was the baby then, born in April. In May or June, Mrs. Mathewson came over, and she told Mama, "You can't have that pretty little baby in the barn. Kaia can come over to my house and stay. Send the diapers and the baby bottle. Kaia can take care of her at my house." She had a nice house; it was immaculate. There was no electricity, and they had a well outside, but it was nice. I stayed over there and took care of my little sister while her husband was building the house for the folks. I was thirteen.

The first year at Swan Crick, we had to go to school in the summertime. It was so far to go, about a mile and a half. It was the poor people's kids that went to this schoolhouse, three of us and four others. The rich people sent their kids to school in town.

We'd walk in the fall of the year when the weather was good. In the winter, the snow got real deep. Sometimes we would stay home because of the cold and the snow. It seemed in those years we'd get three or four feet of snow.

Dad put us on a horse one time, and he said, "Don't get into a coulee, stay on the hillside. If you get into a coulee, the horse'll get stuck."

Somehow or other we *did* get into a coulee, and the horse got stuck and stayed there. We got off the horse and walked the rest of the way to school. A blizzard came up, a terrible blizzard. Dad thought he'd better come get us at school. On the way, he discovered the horse in the snowdrift. He got him out, then he came down to the schoolhouse. I remember it was so cold and the wind was blowing so hard he was afraid we'd freeze to death. We had to walk, and he broke the trail with the horse.

Although the Liens' life was, by our standards, one of hard work and privation, Kaia and her siblings were happy children.

Mother sewed all of our clothes by hand. Every fall Dad would go to town and buy a bolt of material. She'd cut out dresses. My sisters and I had dresses made alike, of the same material, and we were happy to get those. When we came home from school, we would change our clothes. We had one pair of shoes at a time. The funny part was, we never felt poor. It never came to us that we were poor. Everybody was in the same circumstances.

We bought our underwear, but Mother knitted all the stockings, all the mittens we wore. When she knitted, she never looked at her knitting. She knitted stockings and mittens up until she died.

All the time we were in the grades, we had knitted stockings. And I was allergic to wool.

My mother said, "Kaia's the fussiest thing! She's fussing about those nice woolen stockings."

I said, "They make me itch."

She said, "I don't understand that."

The Lien children were taught to work from the time they could walk, although Kaia felt it had been a blessing over the years.

I must have been nine or ten when Mama gave me a bucket and said, "Go out and milk the cow." I wasn't so good to start with. Mama didn't milk; it was up to us kids to do the milking. It was one of those things that had to be done. At nine or ten, I was washing clothes on the washboard.

Mama kept having babies. I had to help take care of them all the time. When I was supposed to be in the sixth grade, Dad said, "You'll have to stay home and help Mother. Maybe you can start Thanksgiving." That year I did get to start at Thanksgiving. Next year it was the same thing. You know how hard it is to start in the middle of the term.

My brother, Sam, had to quit school when he was in the sixth grade because he had to go to work.

The following year Dad said, "You can't start school now because Mama needs you." I helped Mama all I could, and I did most of the baking. I sewed; I made dresses for my younger sisters. That year, when I was supposed to be in the eighth grade, I never got to go to school at all.

I kept thinking, "I'll have to get away from home or I'll never get an education. This is going to be my life, and I'll have to marry the first guy that comes along." My dad didn't believe in women having an education. They didn't need it; they just got married. All the old people were like that.

Well, in March a woman up at Melville advertised for a housekeeper in the *Big Timber Pioneer*. I sat down and wrote a letter, said I'd like to apply for her house-keeping job. I was fifteen.

When the mailman came next morning, I sent my letter. The following morning at six o'clock the telephone rang; a woman wanted to talk to Kaia. She said she'd got my letter. She wanted me to come up with the mailman. They'd meet me in Melville. The mailman delivered the mail from Big Timber to Melville, and he took passengers back and forth in a double-seated buggy with a team of horses.

I was real excited. I had a few clothes, and I put them in a box. I was just going out the door when my dad came in.

"What's all the commotion?"

Mama said, "Kaia's going off to Melville to work for the Harts."

"How'd you find out about that?"

I said, "There's an ad in the *Pioneer*."

"Where's the *Pioneer*?"

The kids ran and got it for him. He looked through the ad and said, "A *woman*. You're not a woman. You're a little kid, and a skinny one at that."

"Well," I said, "she wants me."

I was quite a ways off in the yard when he yelled at me. "If you don't get twenty dollars a month, you come back home."

The Harts were so good to me. Whatever I did, they praised me. She said, "I'm going to pay you fifteen dollars a month."

I started to cry. "Dad said if I didn't get twenty dollars a month, I'd have to come home."

"Well," she said, "if you can do the wash, I'll give you twenty dollars a month."

Every Monday morning I got up at 4 o'clock. I had the washing out on the line before I had to get breakfast.

She didn't have a washing machine. She had two big tubs and one of those plungers. You plunged the wash, but you wrung it out by hand. They had four or five hired men and sometimes company from back East. I had all those sheets and pillowcases to wash and extra meals [for the houseguests]. And ironing! Great baskets of ironing! But I loved to iron, so that wasn't any problem.

The Harts ate in one part of the house, the hired help in another. I had to get a good substantial breakfast for the hired men. I cooked oatmeal, hotcakes, eggs, and coffee. At home we had to be so careful not to use too much sugar or butter and cream. I was in my glory up there. I could use all the butter, all the sugar, all the cream I wanted, and I did!

For the first time in my life, I realized the folks were poor. Real poor. Our table manners at home weren't that good, so Mrs. Hart taught me table manners and other manners.

She kept me busy. I'd work as fast as I could and have everything done up. There'd be a little time in the afternoon, and she'd give me a spade. I'd have to go out and dig dandelions out of the yard. I was busy every second. But I learned so much that was good for me. And I was happy.

Mrs. Hart let me go to church every Sunday. I could walk across the field to the Melville Lutheran church [the oldest Lutheran church in Montana].

During the summer I wrote letters to the eighth-grade principal in Big Timber, asking him if he could find a place for me to work for my board and room because I wanted to take up the eighth grade in town. He found a place. I worked for my room and board while I was going to the eighth grade. And they were really nice people.

When school started, I bought a new pair of shoes and a new coat. I bought a skirt, and I made two blouses.

The next year I went to high school. I worked for my room and board with Beulah Patterson. They had a hardware store. She had four children, three little girls upstairs and the baby in the cradle. I'd sit and study at night, diaper the baby and feed him. Then the girls upstairs, "I'm cold! I don't have any covers on!" I'd go up and cover them, and after a little bit, "Kaia, I'm thirsty. I want a drink." Up the stairs I'd go. This was the way it went. But they were good to me.

Math was hard for me because the way I went to school, I never got the beginning of anything. Mr. Patterson helped me with my algebra and my geometry. Once in a while, Mrs. Patterson would say, "Let me read your English," and there'd be something that she'd discover and tell me about.

My English teacher was tall; she had black hair and eyes, and she'd look right through you. She asked a question that Beulah had explained to me. Nobody knew the answer but me. She said, "Here this girl is working for her room and board. She doesn't run around at night having fun like you kids do, and she always has her lessons."

I tell you, I felt so good. The Pattersons really helped me.

After Kaia's first school year in Big Timber, Mrs. Hart offered her summer work, this time only three days a week. Kaia declined, saying, "I'm on my own; I have a hard enough time to get along when I work full-time." She found full-time work that summer at the Franklin Ranch near Melville. Until she graduated from high school, Kaia alternated working summers for Mrs. Franklin with working for Mrs. Patterson in Big Timber during the school term.

There were ten men to cook for, but they had their dining room, and Mrs. Franklin and I ate in the kitchen.

She did her own wash. All I had to do was cook for those men, keep the dining room and the kitchen nice and clean. I got along with her real good.

They had a great big kitchen. The men filled the wood box from the outside. A ditch went under the kitchen floor and down the field, sparkling clear water from Sweet Grass Crick. They had built a log cabin onto their house; that was my room. The ditch went right past my bedroom. At night it was so tranquil.

There was a big cookstove. It had a warming oven and a tank where the water was heated. There were big cupboards and a hardwood floor. I used to scrub that floor until it was shining.

I got up at 5. Breakfast at 6, dinner at 12, supper at 6.

Up at the Harts she explained to me that if you had rice you didn't need potatoes, because they were both starch. I thought I'd get the men a treat, so I cooked a big kettle of fluffy rice one day. I put it on the table with their steaks and their gravy and vegetables. I poured their coffee 'n' everything. They just sat there. Just sat there. Finally Mr. Franklin said, "WHERE ARE THE POTATOES?"

"I didn't cook any potatoes. That rice is starch, and you aren't supposed to have two starches at one meal. Potatoes are a starch, so I thought it'd be a change."

"From now on, POTATOES. Three times a day!"

Those hired men, they teased me from then on about starch. That was the first time they'd ever heard there was starch in potatoes and rice.

They had fried potatoes for breakfast, bacon and eggs and ham, hotcakes and biscuits. They liked those biscuits with jam. I served meat three times a day. They drank coffee with all their meals. They were big meals, all of them.

At noon there'd be meat, potatoes and gravy, a vegetable, bread, and dessert of some kind. They had balanced meals. They were hardworking people. Sometimes I would cook enough potatoes for dinner that I would warm them over for supper or fry them.

There were wild raspberry bushes. I would go out and pick raspberries, then I'd make raspberry shortcake with whipped cream. Mrs. Franklin said I was the only girl who ever bothered to go out and pick raspberries. And they had a garden, so I had a lot of nice vegetables. A hired man worked in the garden.

The ditch ran through the springhouse [where the food was kept cool]. They had drawers or bins where you'd put milk and cream and different things.

Up at Melville the ranchers would butcher a beef, and they would divide it up. The Franklins had a little house made of mosquito netting out in the brush where the sun never hit it. It was screened tight so no flies or anything got in. It didn't get warm in the shade during the day, and the nights were nice and cool. When the meat was gone, some other rancher would butcher a beef and bring [a portion] to the Franklins. That's the way they worked it. There was always a lot of nice fresh meat.

One of Mr. Franklin's young hired men invited Kaia to accompany him to a local Saturday night dance.

He had a new little Bluebird car. I said, "I'd like to go, but I don't know if I can." I asked Mrs. Franklin. She said, "Honey, you don't want to go up there. They get drunk up there. You don't want to go to that dance."

"Couldn't I just go up and look on for a while, and if I don't like it, why, Helmer said he'd take me home. Whenever I want to go home, he'll take me." She let me go then.

I had a marvelous time. Here I was, a new girl, I didn't know how to dance, and do you know, all those boys asked me to dance. The next day Mrs. Franklin was asking me everything that took place. She had as much fun as I did. And so I went . . . every time they had a dance. Some of the boys were wild, but I was with a nice bunch. I just love to dance. . . .

Kaia kept her spunkiness throughout her life, as evidenced by the story she tells about her "search for the missing calf" when she was eighty-one.

One morning Frank [Kaia's son] said, "I think your black cow calved last night, but I can't find the calf."

I thought if she'd calved, she'd go on the island [in Otter Creek] and have it over there. I put on my over-shoes because it was snowy, muddy, and cold and a coat that came down to my knees. There was a tree [lying] across the crick, and the crick was awfully high. I started across on this log, and I'll be blessed if I didn't fall into the crick! And I can't swim. Every branch I tried to get ahold of came into the crick with me. It was a really deep hole there, under a high bank. And it was in this same hole that a calf had once drowned.

All the time I kept thinking, "If I drown in Otter Crick, nobody will ever find me. Frank wouldn't think of looking in the crick for me." I held on to the tree with one hand. I must have somehow or other climbed up on the tree. To this day, I don't know how I got out. I really don't. My clothes were covered with dirty foam; everything was sopping wet. I came in and took a bath and put on dry clothes. Next day she had her calf up in the field.

A young woman to whom Kaia told the tale of the missing calf said, "I wouldn't have crossed that crick if every calf on the ranch had drowned." Throwing up her hands, Kaia said, "See the difference? I was used to saving everything so we could live. . . ."

Kaia Cosgriff was interviewed at her home in Sweet Grass County, Montana, in January 1987. When she died in Big Timber in February 1999, she was some four months shy of her one-hundredth birthday.

LILLIAN MOLINE MEHLHOFF

*"A basket of white eggs,
there's just nothing hardly prettier."*

Lillian Mehlhoff was born on May 4, 1927, and grew up along-
side her two brothers and three sisters in Brantford, North
Dakota. Even as a child, she kept chickens, and by adulthood
she had developed an expertise in poultry raising that gives
her a certain status, a status she enjoys. Lillian is pleasantly
plump. She has short, curly brown hair, blue eyes, and a rapid
manner of speaking. At home, she is never without her apron.
She laughs a lot and tends to make light of things. Her religion
is important to her.

I had a very good mother and a very good dad. My
father, if we did something we weren't supposed to do,
if we weren't honest, we were punished. I remember
my dad teaching me: You do not take anything that is
not yours. I remember so plain, I had run across the

pasture to the schoolhouse and found, in a junk pile, some lignite coal. I took an old pail off the junk pile, and I filled this pail—just a little pail—with coal that was there. Why the coal was there, I don't know. I brought it home, and I thought, oh, I've done such a good thing! I set it beside the cookstove.

When my dad came in, he asked my mother, "Where did that coal come from?" My mother said, "Nooks found it on Andersons' junk pile." He says, "Nooks, you take that right back." I took it back. That taught me a lot.

My father passed away when we were young. The youngest one was twelve. It's hard to run a household without a father. It's hard to run it without a mother, but when the Lord takes one or the other, you make out as good as you can. I suppose I give my mother more credit that way, for her faithfulness, her love, her prayers. She was a praying woman. I guess I wouldn't be what I am today if it weren't for my mother.

All of us kids raised chickens when we were young. We got to have the money, the proceeds from selling the chickens. We had the heavy breeds, the meat breeds. There were Buff Orpingtons, Red Rhode Island, Wyandotte. We stuck to those heavy breeds because we wanted to use some for meat. Heavy breeds wouldn't be as good a layer by far, but we'd get enough eggs for our family.

We used our eggs to set hens, so there was no cost in it. Got the feed from our dad, fed 'em what we raised. We would probably have about three or four hens. If the hatch was good, we kept a lot of roosters, from ten to fourteen. We would eat some of them; some we sold to Swift's. We took them to our town, fourteen miles away, and they'd pay us cash.

Of course, we always had a list a mile long, what we were going to do with this money, and the money never went around. You know how it is with kids. We'd buy clothes and things that were useful. This is a good thing, to teach a child the value of money when they earn their own.

We would save up some money, and we would order chickens from the Swift Company. Swift had an outlet in New Rockford [North Dakota]; they sold chickens, bought eggs, and bought the poultry. I remember the money that we got for each chicken we sold. I don't think it was much over a dollar. It depended on how big we let them get. Us kids would wait as long as we could. The more they weighed, the more we'd get. It wasn't that much, but if you had twenty chickens, that was twenty dollars, and in those days twenty dollars was quite a bit.

Later, when we got older, we went into the egg business. We bought and raised pullets [young hens], and we'd sell the eggs year-round. We went into the Leghorn [breed]. They're strictly for laying, not for meat. The cheapest I remember eggs sold for was twenty-five cents a dozen. Just guessing, I s'pose in 1947.

After Lillian married Lawrence Mehlhoff, the couple moved to the Paradise Valley in Montana, where Lillian continued to love her chickens.

A lot of people have preference to the white egg. And then we have the people who want the brown egg. Some figure if it's a brown egg, it's no good. Don't know where they got their theory from. White egg, a lot of people like them for dyeing for Easter.

Myself, it really doesn't make any difference. You have to clean the white eggs more. They still show *every speck* where a brown egg won't.

A basket of white eggs, there's just nothing hardly prettier.

When I got my pullets this fall, they were ready to lay and not used to roosts. I suppose they'd been in cages. When I turned them loose in my henhouse, not one of them would roost. They all crowded in a corner, and we lost one. Luckily that was all we lost. The [hatchery] fellow told us, "They're going to have to learn to roost." And yet today—that's two months now—there are some of them, a few of them, that don't roost yet. They still crowd in that little corner but not enough to kill each other. It depends on how you raise them, see? You know how, in these big companies that raise a lot of chickens for laying, they don't let them out and they're not in buildings like mine here; they're in cages. They raise them in cages, in stacks. Mine are real fortunate, they get to go outside.

I let my chickens out, depending on the weather, in a month. Depends on what kind of chickens they are. For the broilers, no. I keep them penned so the meat is tenderer. For the pullets, you like to have them to get out and get their grit. It's good for them. It's even good for the laying hens to run around. Your egg yolks are nice and orange, just a much better egg than when they're cooped up. This is why your eggs are pale and white when they're in cages and don't get all the nutrients they pick up on the ranch. The yolks are white like the white! You scramble them or do anything else with them, it's just no good.

I've had compliments on my eggs. I tell you, I have no problem at all to get a dollar a dozen. No, I don't. Even pullet eggs.

I have sold eggs to the health food stores, and their requirements were: fertile eggs and the chickens to run outdoors. They told me fertile eggs and running outdoors is less cholesterol. Now, I don't know. I haven't backed it up. But that's what the health food store told me.

I remember when we were raising chicks ourselves, there with the cluck [mother hen], you would have to keep them in the house until she was done. But they were really not that much mess. You just kept them in a little box, covered up, in any corner, anyplace that was warm. Chickens like it warm, very warm. Feed them every two hours until they're all hatched. If you let her have the babies, then she would leave her nest and leave the rest of the eggs, and you wouldn't get all the chickens.

I do that yet today. You pick up the little ones every morning and every night and bring them in. You wait until [the hen's] got the last egg hatched, and *then* you give her the chicks. Then she's happy.

When Lillian's chicks were "tiny babes," she kept them, in the absence of mother hens, in a brooder house. The brooder house, a metal, canopied enclosure within the henhouse, afforded warmth and protection to the fledgling chicks. She went on to describe the henhouse itself.

It's a two-room henhouse. There's so much room, I could have another hundred in there. I'll close off half of it if it should get to forty below. With that many chickens in the room, they produce their own heat. If you need heat, put a bulb, a heat lamp above your waterer. Last year, very, very few times did the waterer freeze over. And that was when it was forty below and the wind was blowing. I don't know how it's going to be this year. We'll find out, won't we?

Chickens love sun. When the sun comes out in the morning, they're all sitting where the sun's shining in through the windows. They like the warmth. A chicken can stand a lot of heat, but dampness is not good for them. They get colds, plugged-up nostrils, I guess you'd call it. It's not healthy. . . .

I think if a chicken's too cold, it won't lay. They have to be comfortable. If you throw some grain, some whole barley on the floor, give them something to do, to scratch, keep them busy, that warms them up. The whole grain stays in their gizzard longer, and this produces heat. This is good in the wintertime. If you grind your feed real fine, it goes through the gizzard faster, and it doesn't produce as much heat. So, a chicken will keep warmer on the whole grain than on the ground, fine grain.

You never have predator problems when you have a cement floor. I think one of your worst predators would be the weasel. They can come through the smallest hole and do tons of damage. I have seen, when I was small, where a weasel would kill a hundred baby chicks in one night. They're wicked. Or a mink. They'll get in a hen-house and do lots of damage, too. Neither one of these creatures eats the meat; they just suck the blood.

I have a lot of eagles around here, a lot of hawks, and I have a lot of owls, but to this day I don't know that they have ever gotten any chickens. I think maybe because my chickens have a good cover. There's this big sloping barn; we used it for sheep. As long as they're under cover, they can't get them. Eagles and hawks are bad on chickens. Nothing to fool with. . . .

There are other things that happen, too. Chickens are great fowls to eat each other, pick each other. There you use your home remedy. A good thing for that is to put a weigh block in among them so they have something to do. Then they quit. It has salt in it, some vitamins. They eat that instead of picking each other.

When they're just tiny babes to full grown, I think you may lose ten out of a hundred, 10 percent. But I've lots of times raised better than that. I like my chickens, and I like to be around them. I care for them the best way I know how.

You can tell [healthy chicks] by their feathers, if they're shiny and bright. Hearty appetite, not sitting around, always on the go. Yes, very active. And then they will sleep. They're always eating and drinking and sleeping, like a [human] infant.

Your heat. Water. Good feed. You've got those three, chickens survive.

Lillian hastens to describe the world of the chicken—the hierarchy, the different personalities, the maternal instincts.

It's kind of a novelty, this banty hen business. You put one [banty] with fifty or sixty chickens, they can't make it. Even with the roosters. It's very interesting. When they brought these pullets, I had roosters that I'd raised. I waited for about two weeks, then I put one rooster in. All these pullets, they went after him and picked him and were ready to fight him. He picked them; he was very stern with them. He had to be the top one in that henhouse. When they knew that, they left him alone. I waited another week; I put another rooster in. He had to do the same thing. You get too many roosters in there; you can't do that, either.

I think they have a personality, like a dog or a cat or anything else. This noon when I went in to get the eggs, I opened the door, and this old hen, she kind of squawked. Just that one particular hen. Told me "hello," I guess. Sometimes they'll show you they're hungry. When they lay their egg, they'll tell you by cackling. You have to like these animals to notice this. I think an animal knows when you like them. You tell this to some people, they [think] that's impossible.

There are lots of ways you can make a pet out of chickens. Spending time with them, holding them, being around them a lot.

You think [chickens are] kind of ignorant, but really, when they hide their nests away, they want to be secluded. They lay an egg every day, and then they sit on it and nest. Mother Nature. They take care of those little babies off the nest and see that they get water and feed. I've seen hens hide their nests away and come off with thirteen or fourteen baby chicks and raise them all. So I don't think they can be that ignorant. Very good mothers. . . .

I've seen roosters getting food for their hens, all the time. They will scratch, and then they call the chicken over to give up whatever they found. Lots of times, I've seen them, too, probably didn't find anything, calling them over. One way of communicating for chickens.

There's always one rooster that is *the boss*. Right now, I have four roosters in my henhouse, and one of those is the boss. And then there's one step down; he chases the other two. And the next one will chase the last one, and the last one is the poor rooster that hasn't got anyone to chase, and he runs from all three of them. Roosters will kill. They fight to kill. If you get a real bossy one, he wants to be the *only* [rooster]. You can't have that. He gets the axe!

A healthy hen will molt once a year, in the fall. A molt is when a chicken loses its feathers. They stop laying; they will lose all their feathers and then start in over again making new feathers for their bodies. Takes approximately a month. Depends on how you feed them. You should feed them well so they get the nutrients to grow another nice batch of feathers. A hen, when it's done molting, looks like a new hen!

Lillian's instructions for butchering and preparing a chicken for the pot cover every detail.

My way of butchering chickens is pen them up, catch them in the evening when you can catch them easily, put them in a crate, and in the morning butcher them. That way they don't have any feed in their crops, and they're much easier to dress.

I myself don't kill them. My husband does, my daughter does, my sons do. We catch them and hang them up, take a butcher knife and cut the head off. That way they do not flop around in the dirt and they don't get dirty. It's just a nice clean job. You put them in a wheelbarrow or a tub, whatever you want to take them to the house with. Then you scald them. I use a five-gallon pail. An old hen, you use boiling water, and you don't have to be real careful. You hardly ever overscald an old hen. With younger ones, you have to be very careful. You can't use boiling water. You have to add cold to it so you don't overscald, or when you pull the feathers, the skin comes off.

I cook [chickens] with the skin on. However, when I make soup, I never make [it] the same day as I boil my hen. I take it off the bones, then I cool it, set it in the refrigerator, skim off the fat, and throw [the skin] away. But the flavor is there, in the broth. I don't have the fat. I don't need the fat.

I pluck chickens wet. First you take the wing feathers, the tail feathers, because those are the hardest to get out. Then if you take your hand and roll it right on down towards the head, starting from the back, you can roll the feathers right off. If they don't have any pinfeathers, it doesn't take more than a couple of minutes to take the feathers off. If you have pins, you can spend hours on them. Especially if they're black. Your black pinfeather will show, where a light pinfeather won't.

Now you have your chicken defeathered. Then I singe them. I use rubbing alcohol. I put it in a little lid and light it, and you burn the hair off the chicken. Then I wash them. I use Ivory soap and a brush. After I get it washed, I leave it laying for a while, and then I dress it.

Take the crop and windpipe out, and then from the back, you take the intestines out. And then, it depends on what you want to do with that chicken. If you want to fry it, if it's a young one, you cut it up right then. Wash it again, or leave it in water. I usually let it lay in water for several hours. Cool, take the body heat out. When that's done, why then you can cut it up into pieces, and you've got your chicken, ready to cook.

The difference in flavor between my chickens and store-bought, well, I can tell you what other people tell me: HUGE *big* difference. I don't buy store-bought chicken. I think I've bought them once in my life.

Lillian had raised chickens her entire life but had only recently branched out to turkeys.

I started out with fourteen turkeys, and I ended up with eight or nine. I buy them from the hatchery, a day old, just hatched. Two dollars and twenty-five, two dollars and fifty cents. . . .

The manager of the hatchery told me this year, "If you can raise 60 percent of your turkeys, you're doing a good job." Now with chickens, the percentage is much higher than that. Ten percent [loss] is not too bad. Lots of times you can raise 100 percent. If you lose two out of a hundred, that's real good, but ten, I suppose that's average.

Turkeys, why are they harder to raise? Maybe more diseases, get diseases easier. They're like sheep; they don't care, they just die. If they're sick, they die. They think they should die. Being I've done it two years, I know what I'd do next year. Just as soon as I brought them home from the hatchery, I'd give them some Terramycin. Terramycin will take care of just about anything they have. What I lost mine from this year was pneumonia. It was the coldest day in May, and they died real fast. The hatchery didn't know what was wrong with them. Had no idea what was wrong with them until I sat down and watched these little turkeys. I saw they were gasping for air. Didn't take long, maybe in a day they die. They do get pneumonia, but you can treat it. Treat it with Terramycin. That was it. Once I got over that, I didn't lose any more.

Chickens and turkeys should not be housed together. You read any book, they'll tell you not to raise chickens with turkeys. Not to have them on the same ground. I've done this: not housed at night in the same building, but they went over the same ground the chickens did [during the day].

Turkeys like to roost out. If you don't have rodents around to get your turkey, fine, but they're much safer under the barn roof. They go as high as they can [to] roost. They'll fly up to the roof of the barn and roost overnight.

I feed mine barley, barley and oyster shells. They have their grit outside. I never fed mine fancy at all. Fed them turkey mash or turkey scratch until they were about a month old, and then I put them on barley. Rolled barley, whole barley, anything. Barley's good. It fattens them nice for roasting. For roasting you have to have some fat.

There were several people who wanted turkeys, but I had bad luck just before I butchered my turkeys this year. The fellow that ground our hay was having trouble; antifreeze was getting into his engine. He drained it all out at our place and left the bucket of antifreeze sit there. Who do you suppose came and drank that antifreeze but five of my turkeys. Well, to make a long story short, it killed them.

The vet says the antifreeze is sweet, tastes good. A turkey will try anything. They'll pick at anything. And drink it! What it does, it destroys their kidneys, and they die from toxins. . . .

I still had nine left. Nine out of fourteen. My heaviest one was twenty-two pounds. My lightest was eleven. I noticed when I butchered the small one, her heart was deformed. Possibly that's why she was so small.

Chickens are probably cheaper to raise. You can take care of more of them; you can sell your chickens or sell your eggs. But on the whole, a turkey is more interesting to raise than a chicken. If you have a car or any vehicle sitting around, [turkeys] are on top of it. You leave the truck open, they're inside it; tractors, they're on it. They're really nuisances! They'll come up to the house, sit on the porch, eat the strawberries, and . . . they're bad. They like to be with people. I had to laugh, just a couple of days before Thanksgiving, they came up on my step, and they looked in through the window. They were standing there, and they had no idea they were so close to the dinner table.

They're friendly, and should we say stupid? When we killed them, why, we caught them right in the barn. You can pick them up, and Lawrence would hang them right by our feet. They have no idea they're next. No fear. None whatever.

With us, our barn is a long way from the house, which is nice. But eventually they find the house. We trained the two dogs that the turkeys are not supposed to be in the yard. Otherwise, they'd live in the yard, just like geese. Geese are the same way. I think they like to be around people.

You can get mean gobblers, too. They can be *really* mean. I've heard of adults being afraid of them, and if there's little children around, they can hurt them very badly. They fight with their feet and their claws. And their wings! You get hit with a wing, you'd be surprised at the force behind that. Wouldn't think it unless you got hit.

By the end of the interview, Lillian can't help but go back to talking about her chickens.

I like [raising chickens] not so much because it gives me something to do—not that I can't find anything to do—but I know if I didn't have chickens in the wintertime, I probably wouldn't even go outside during the day. This way, I get fresh air, my exercise. I enjoy doing it, and while I am able to do it, I would like to.

When us kids were raising chickens, you could buy a pair of shoes for a dollar, and we would buy school clothes. And now, I use [chicken and egg money] for groceries, for the telephone bill. I use it for church and Sunday School and stamp books. Not that you get a lot of it, but it's a source of money where you have change in your purse all the time. You can't pay a big bill with it or something like that.

Years ago, you could buy all your groceries. [Having an income] gives you a great satisfaction. Now like with my egg money, it's something I don't have to get out of some other source. I can do things with it that I otherwise wouldn't ever do.

Lillian Mehlhoff was interviewed in December 1986 at her kitchen table in her home on the Yellowstone River in Paradise Valley. The youngest of the women interviewed here—she is a generation younger than some of the others—she lives today in Twin Bridges, Montana, not far from a son and daughter-in-law.

ETHEL GOUDY BRIGGS

"I intend to milk as long as I'm able."

Born at home on November 21, 1910, to homesteaders Herbert and Mabel Goudy, Ethel Briggs lived all of her life near Mill Creek in Park County, Montana. She was a small, compactly built woman, bright, alert, and good-humored. In 1985, at the time of our conversation, she milked cows twice a day, baked bread, churned butter, raised a garden, and canned its produce. In her spare time, she made quilts—wild, wonderful things of diverse pattern and color.

Ethel and her husband, Leo, eventually sold their ranch to neighbors, reserving a lifetime interest in their home. They could have sold their property to a developer at a greatly inflated price, but they chose instead to ask a price that made it possible for their young buyers to keep the ranch in agricultural production.

Father took over a partly settled homestead. I believe it was in 1906 that he finished up, went to the courthouse in town [Livingston], and got his claim proved up. There was a small house there to begin with. When they built the rest, I'm not sure. It was there when I was born. In November of 1910, Father finished building a large cistern on the side of the hill. He piped the water down to the house so they had running water. They also had it piped to a big tank behind the Majestic stove. In wintertime we used coal to hold the fire longer; in the summertime we used wood.

Like many families at the time, the Goudys used various home remedies to treat illnesses.

In the old days they had to be awf'lly sick before they'd go to a doctor. My folks had great faith in the medicinal properties of sassafras tea, a drink they fixed in the spring to clear our blood. It wasn't too bad, but there was . . . what was that terrible thing called? Assidity or something like that. And it stunk! We had to wear it on our chest when we had a cold. That word is away back there; I can't bring it to mind. [The word Briggs was searching for is "acifidity."]Probably it just encouraged us to get to feeling better so we didn't have to wear it.

Among Ethel's earliest memories are those of learning to ride horses with her father.

When I was a baby, Father would get the nursing bottle, some diapers, and a pillow, and he'd take me irrigating. A neighbor lady said, "That man is gonna kill that baby!" She just knew it. He started me riding horseback before I was able to set up on the horse. When he took the cattle up to the mountains, or went after the cattle, take them salt, I was always along.

I couldn't have been more than five when I got my first horse. My legs just barely stuck out on each side of the horse. Father had to cut the sides of the saddle so's to get the stirrups up high enough for my feet.

One time Father gave Frieda [Ethel's sister] a colt, and finally she wanted him broke. He was getting pretty close to being a four-year-old. We went up in the pasture, and we put a saddle on him. I didn't lead him anyplace; I just plain got on. He took off in a straight line for the crick. We got pretty close to the edge of the hill, and I thought, "We've got to change directions here." I patted him on the side, and he turned and galloped clear around and back up to the other end of the field. By then he was beginning to get over being afraid. He never offered to buck. Father . . . oh dear, he was proud!

I tell you, it was years after he was gone, I would be washing the dishes here at the sink, I'd look down the road and wish I could see him riding his horse up the lane.

When I was a girl, families made their own entertainment. We did so much more visiting then. They went by team and wagon or team and buggy. They visited more than we do nowadays with cars. Quite often, if it was a little far off, they'd go and spend the night.

After I grew up, there were dances. They had so many dances around here. Dances up at Chico Springs, over at Emigrant, and at the Mill Creek Flat School. The Busby boys were good musicians and always played. They never charged. Oh, we'd have the best time! It lasted until at least three o'clock in the morning. Never thought of going home at midnight.

Usually we went by car, but I've been to several dances horseback. We went to Emigrant horseback; that's five miles. We went up to Six Mile School, and that would be around ten miles. I did that twice. You are so tired when you start home you could almost die, and then riding horseback!

They had refreshments at all the dances. The womenfolks would bring sandwiches or cake. Whoever was on the committee would have coffee and that.

There was about forty of us in this whole valley that used to go on picnics and horseback rides, and we all went to the same dances. I missed out on one horseback ride they took up Mill Crick and circled around. They came out at Six Mile. I wouldn't have any idea how many miles that would be, but it's a long old ride. My sister was along with the bunch of them, and she said there was some of those poor girls, they couldn't hardly stand to set by the time they got clear around.

Ethel married Leo Briggs, the boy next door, when she was twenty-one, and she went right to work on the ranch.

We lived over the hill from where we live now. The house, all the buildings, are gone. We did move the barn over; we have it for a hay barn. The first story [of the barn] was all laid up in rocks; the top was boards. We got Mr. Percival to move the board part over here. He moved it, set it up where we wanted it, right against the cow barn.

After that, Leo hauled in quite a bit of rock. I rocked the foundation. I loved to lay up those rocks. I had very few fall down, and I didn't have all flat rock a-tall. Round ones, ill-shaped ones, I found you had to have each one perfectly solid. If it rocked, it wouldn't work. It'd throw the rest off so they'd eventually fall down. After we got the barn rocked up, we cemented it.

I look at all that work and think, "I wouldn't want to have a thing to do with it now." Lifting those boulders, they were such heavy things; I don't know how I've got any back that hangs together at all.

Anything that was movable, I moved it. That's one reason my back isn't quite as good as it should be. A few times, when I got disgusted with my old cow, I practically picked up her rear end with my shoulder when I was milking her. Oh, there's lots of things. I felt sorry for a yearling we couldn't keep home. Leo kept her inside the shed. I lifted a big old five-gallon bucket clear over my head to get to where she was.

That was the starter of my recent back trouble. I had to have a few treatments during the year. This winter the chiropractor took off at Thanksgiving. I thought, "What am I going to do?"

I got this little ball, about the size of a golf ball, and I put it down on the floor. I roll it back and forth, up and down my back. When I'm doing heavy lifting, I do it every day. It's keeping my back okay.

When I get working outside, I realize I can't take it like I used to. I have to come in and stretch out on the couch and rest for fifteen or twenty minutes; then I can go back and do some more. When I start something, I'm a fright; I want to finish it.

I don't think as young as I used to. There's one thing: If I could roll the years back, I wouldn't go back to the teens. I think that's the most awful period of anyone's life.

If I could choose an age . . . maybe around forty. I could do anything I wanted to; nothing ever seemed to bother me. I got tired, but it isn't like when you get to be seventy-four. I guess the only way to describe it is, you get bone-tired.

You'll hear young people say, "Yes, I know what you mean." They don't know a thing about it. They get tired, yes, but a little rest, and they're off and going again. It don't soak through your muscles down to the bones like it does when you get to be in your seventies.

When Mother was around sixty, she was rather feeble. Goodness, I got to be sixty and didn't think a thing about it. I think most people are staying young longer. But then you run across some that gets old young. If you're around young people, it makes a big difference.

In her young married years, Ethel and several other women in the area started a birthday club.

To begin with, we would go to each person's house when their birthday come due, sort of on the order of a surprise until it got to be common. I know one time when I had them, I made cinnamon rolls. I don't know how many rolls I made, but a great big old pan just fit in the oven, and I took it out twice. The rest of them that came brought potluck. The hostess would fix coffee and lemonade and have rolls.

Then they started making quilts, and it wasn't too long 'til we were making birthday quilts. Each one would make a block. You were supposed to put your name and your age on it, or the year you were born. I remember one woman, she was an older woman but didn't want to admit it. She never put her age on a-tall, so when I made my block for her, I didn't put my age on it either. That was the way of it.

There were . . . I'll bet one's in the bottom of the cedar chest. If I could get ahold of it, I'd show it to you. They had flowers, birds, or whatever embroidered on them. After we got it all together, we'd quilt it.

We have a meeting now and then. It's pretty seldom. Seven or eight of us, that's all that's left in the club.

Ethel's spunk and sense of humor were especially evident when she talked of her hunting experiences.

I got buck fever the first time I went out hunting alone. I barely got away from my horse when I saw this great big buck, and there was a doe and a yearling with him. I thought, "I can't load the big one nor the middle one alone; I'll pick off the little one." I got up there, and pang, pang, pang, I kept quivering. I was so disgusted with myself I went back to the horse and came home. I hadn't touched a thing. I started pulling the trigger before I even got it aimed. I was so ashamed of myself that I just plain came home. Forgot about it for that day.

Another time I saw, 'way down the mountain . . . it looked like a monster . . . can't be a deer. I kept looking and looking and fooling around. Finally he could feel me. Up he went on the mountain. He had the most terrific rack; I couldn't believe my eyes. I woulda been able to crow if I'd got *him*.

I used to go up the mountain, and as long as I could see something, I didn't care whether I got a shot or not. I would sneak up and keep sneaking, getting a little closer and a little closer. Sometimes I'd get so pesky close I could throw a rock at them before they realized I was there. Afterwards I'd think, "What was the matter with me? I could have had that piece of meat." But I enjoyed myself.

One time I was up Davis Crick. Not too far away there was two little cubs going up a tree, playing and squealing at one another. I looked around for the mama. I couldn't see her, but I sure made tracks.

Another time, at the head of Saw Pit, here was a yearling bear standing up, looking so big. I kept going right on up. I got fairly close, and out of the brush came this fat old mama. Her hide was just a-rolling across her shoulders. She galloped up the hill as fast as she could go, the cubs right after her.

Once when I was leading my horse in very steep country, I saw something I thought was a coyote. I got another glimpse; it was two little cubs. The way the sun was shining on them made them look light-colored. Behind them, hopping over the downfall, came Mama. I thought, "I can't get on my horse; I'll just turn off and hope." As soon as she got a whiff of me, she turned 'round and went the other way. It was all right, but I didn't feel too comfortable for a while.

Ethel seemed to bring the same sense of humor to everything she did, including the myriad ranch chores that needed to be done.

We always had milk cows, and then later we started raising sheep. The coyotes got so bad that Leo finally decided to get out of the sheep business. I was glad, because the last lambing we had, I was so tired, running up and down the hill after medicine or after milk to feed a little lamb. I was bushed. For quite a while after we sold the sheep, we got into cattle. Leo would never butcher any beef for our own use. He felt that it had to be sold to pay expenses, taxes, and so forth.

When I's first married, I used to take a fifteen dozen box of eggs for groceries quite regular. Took 'em over to the Emigrant Store or even to Livingston. We always had to get the gas as well as the groceries out of the eggs and cream. Several times we ran out of gas and had to pack the cream in for a mile or so. Finally, we came to the conclusion that someone was helping to lighten our gas tank. After we got to locking the garage, it helped quite a little bit!

We've always had chickens; we still have eighteen or twenty. I can't think of buying those old store eggs. I don't know how much longer we will raise chickens, but I'd hate to be without a few. You can bake with store eggs; heaven forbid you'd have to eat them!

We're both inclined to make pets of ranch animals. Little pigs can be dreadfully wild when we get them. Leo will scratch their backs and rub their ears when they're busy eating, and it isn't long until they think that feels all right.

He was always quite a hand with the bulls to make them gentle. The horses, all they had to do was nicker at him, and that was good for a fork of hay.

I have always broke all calves to lead so that whenever we keep one, it's halter-broke. Last winter I had to take one to the neighbor's bull. Having to take cows to the bull is a drawback, especially in the wintertime. I led one down to Bob Melin's [a neighbor] behind the Honda three-wheeler and the cart. I asked Leo to put a bale of hay in the back of the cart. I had her tied from the Honda right straight back with a rope so she couldn't come either way. It was ten below that morning. When I got up to the corner, I met the Mill Crick wind. Oh dear, it was cold!

I got down to Bob's, we got the cow taken care of, and we went on in the house. I started to shiver. I didn't think I was ever going to get warmed up. The next morning I went back after the cow, got her up to the mailboxes at the head of the lane, and I turned her loose. She went down the lane quite a ways, then she went over to Paul's fence [next-door neighbor] and bawled. She turned across the road and bawled again. I thought, "I'd better get in the lead." I zoomed on past her. I says, "Come on, Boss," and she followed me right home.

When I was eight or nine, I started milking a cow by myself. I don't mind milking; 'course I never liked to have to do it all by myself. Now Leo sets on the bench watching me, and he's there to pack it to the house.

We used to have to tie these cows up hand and foot. We had one down there; she'd come in the barn, and that tail was just *shhwit, shhwit,* swatting right and left. I's thinking this morning, "My gosh, she don't do that anymore, and I don't have to tie them up."

I know the last time Leo started beatin' the cow down there, I says, "Stop yelling."

"Well, she kicked it over."

I says, "If you'd have had your foot against the bucket, her foot wouldn't have bumped it. She wasn't a-kickin' the bucket; she was just moving her foot ahead."

Well, he was still yelling. "Quit yelling," I says. "You're stirring the whole mess up."

"You're yelling!"

"That's different."

If a cow needs bawling out, I can say one word to her. "Cut it out," or something like that. She'll shake her head. She knows she's being bawled out, but she don't get nervous about it. It don't worry her.

They declare that cattle don't see in color, but you know that's crazy. Heavens to Betsy, you go out there with a different colored coat, and they'll *all* look atcha.

At night we milk at five o'clock, and then in the morning it's whenever. Really odd times. Usually we're down there by seven, but then, they can wait on us if we don't get there at that time.

These days, three cows is all I'm milking because my tendonitis gets to flaring up if I milk any more. We've got two easy cows; the other one isn't so easy, so she's going to have to go down the road this fall. After I milk her, my wrists feel uncomfortable. I have a yearling coming on from the easy milker's side. It's odd—this one that milks hard is a full sister to the one old cow that's so easy to milk. I don't understand that. It has to come through the bull, I guess, to make that difference. We got one calf from Don Clark's [another neighbor] bull, and that heifer is the hardest cow I ever tried to milk! She has such teeny-tiny little holes in her teats that we finally put a calf on her. All of that cow's other calves have been easy to milk.

If I didn't milk cows, there's lots of times when I would go out to Washington and visit my sister and things like that. You can't do that, 'cause there isn't anyone around anymore that can milk cows or would milk cows. I intend to milk as long as I'm able, because in the wintertime I'm afraid I'd get so lazy I'd be in a wheelchair!

It gets—when it's awfully cold—my, but it is miserable to go out and milk a cow, 'specially when it's so cold you have to put your hands up between her bag and her flank to kinda get the frost off the top of your hand. I did that several times this winter. But all in all, I don't mind milking.

In the spirit of independence and economy, Ethel preferred to make her own laundry soap.

I've made soap for years. My recipe says to use the recipe on the lye can, omitting one pound of grease, reducing the amount to five pounds. You dissolve one cup of borax in the grease, two tablespoons of ammonia. Pour the borax and ammonia into the lye, and then you pour this into the grease. Stir continually, but you've got to stir slowly. If you stir too fast, the lye and the grease will separate. It takes about fifteen minutes of stirring before it starts to thicken. I put a dishwiper in the bottom of a wooden box, pour in the soap after it's starting to thicken. I let it set overnight, then I cut it.

It really does clean good. Mostly I use it for washing clothes. I haven't made soap for about three or four years. I had boxes and BOXES of it stored down in the coal bin. I was in hopes it would last me. . . .

I don't know. I guess if I live much longer, I'm going to have to make one more batch.

Despite the hard work and hardships of ranch life, Ethel clearly couldn't imagine living any other way.

I don't think it makes any difference where you live; you'll find disadvantages of one kind or another. For me, there are fewer on the ranch. You have your own meat, your garden stuff, spuds and vegetables, usually fruit. You're more independent, that's the thing. I've always preferred ranch life, even when I was young.

When I have to go to town, I come back home fast as I can. It's going to be a sad day if I ever have to move into town.

Ethel Briggs was interviewed at her home near Mill Creek in March 1985. She died there in April 1998. She was eighty-seven years old.

BEATRICE MCINTYRE MURRAY

"... nuthin' to leave on or nowhere to go."

Beatrice Murray's strong character and independent streak carried her through a difficult life. She was born at Aitkin, Minnesota, on September 24, 1905. The Depression cost the folks their home. They then bought a place out of Pine River, Minnesota, in a little town called Pontoria.

We lived there until the hard times got the best of ya, and the banks went broke. When the bank closed, my dad and mother lost everything they had. Then my father got sick and passed away. About the time the funeral was over with, the bank closed in. We lost the place and had to move.

All the rest of my folks moved up to Duluth, Minnesota, but I went on. I wound up around Roseau [near the Canadian border]. I was up there for a summer.

I came back with some folks, turned out eventually to be my husband's folks.

We got married and lived at Brainerd. We moved into a little place of our own, built out of doors from railroad cars. You could get these doors at the railroad shops in Brainerd. Other folks was doin' the same. We lined up these railroad-car doors, got a roof on, and made a house. After they got the roof on, I put some corrugated pasteboard on the wall to make a little bit of insulation. Then we got wallpaper and papered it. It looked pretty good, but it was far from warm.

When my son was born—it was January 15, 1933, a deep snow, bad weather. I never did get to the hospital. We didn't have the money anyway. He was born right there at home. A neighbor lady come; she'd had some nursing experience. Right toward the last, they got a doctor to come out from Brainerd. I didn't have no baby crib or nothin', so they made a little bed in a big chair we had. My mother came, and she took care of him until I got better.

That's the way we lived. Bake all your bread in a woodstove, do your washing on a washboard. I took in washing from a neighbor boy that was working in the shops. He wasn't married; he'd bring his washing over. I helped us to get along like that. Finally, it got to the WPA [Works Progress Administration] days, and my husband got to be a foreman on one of them crews. That helped out. When them times kinda closed in and broke up, there we sat again with nothin' much to do.

Nothing for a living, not much money coming in. We'd been raisin' a garden while he worked for that WPA.

When we didn't have no work or anything, we got a boxcar from the railroad, piled what stuff we had in there. Russell, my husband, could ride with it, because we had some horses in there that we were going to bring out [to Montana]. My son and I wasn't supposed to be in the boxcar. When it got dark, we went down to the railroad yards; we clumb in and kind of stashed away in there until they got under way. It was a big, long train of stuff. They had one car of pigs that squealed all the way out here. You could hear those squealings forever. Once, the railroad man, he come a-knockin' on the door when we stopped.

"Who've you got in there?"

My husband says, "I's just talkin' to the horses."

"I heard some voices."

"Well, you can get up in here and look if you want to."

By that time, my son and I, we'd scrambled over and got into the manger and threw a little hay over ourselves. The railroad man, his head come up to the bottom of the railroad car where he could look in and see the horses' feet right there.

"I know you've got someone in there," he said, but didn't want to get in and look.

One of them horses got tired of bein' in there, kinda cranky like. He took a bite at one of the other horses and ripped the skin pert near a foot right down his neck. Russell tried to pat it back to place the best he could 'til we got here.

We arrived in Lewistown, then the next day we come out and unloaded at the Roy stockyards. One of the neighbors helped my husband drive the stuff out here. That was in 1940, and we've been here ever since.

My husband had been out before. We had half a section that he'd got with a boy that was stayin' with us back in Minnesota and didn't have no home at that time. My husband bought another half-section; we kept one half, and the boy bought the other half. Land was worth, well, you could buy anything around here for twenty-five, fifty cents an acre. Everybody thought, what's the sense of buyin' it, you might as well just *use* it. There was hardly any grass, hardly any cattle in this area, mostly horses. They'd travel all the way to Roy [several miles] to a little crick to get a drink.

There was no water here, no electricity, no phone. Just an old log house with a door wouldn't shut. The windows was out, and there's a hole in the roof. There's pack rats runnin' along the sides of the logs. You couldn't keep them out; it wasn't solid enough. And dry and hot! Like livin' in the desert. I wondered why in the world would anybody ever want to come here. But we stayed. We didn't have nuthin' to leave on or nowhere to go.

By 1949, my son wanted a room by himself. The house was just a little one-room outfit, so we got another building that we hitched onto it. We built a little place on the back, big enough for a bedroom. It looked like it was going to be neat and kind of nice. We went to town to get some linoleum paste, and we bought a new bedspring and some things to fix it up. When we come back home, the whole place had burned up. Got afire while we were gone.

A neighbor man was livin' right over there. He saw smoke rolling out, and he hurried over here as fast as he could, but it was too far aflame . . . all them old dry logs. He couldn't do anything. He drove clear in to Roy to tell us we better get right out here, our place's all afire.

We'd lost all of our start, everything we had. The neighbor boy bachelor, tryin' to get a start on his place, had left his stuff with us, even his clothes. His clothes and everything burned up, cured hams his folks had given him. Everything! The little old radio we had, run off a car battery. We hadn't had it too long; we's pretty proud of it. Our tools. Gone! We didn't have anything here a-tall.

We burnt out July '49, and we had to have some place before winter. Somebody had some logs they wasn't going to use which was these very logs [in the present house]. My husband had a friend that ran the stage. It come to Roy and delivered the mail, and people would ride it to get to Lewistown. He give Russell some work, and he let him take his truck to go after the logs. I stayed here diggin' out the basement while they were gone. I dug it out best I could until they got back with the logs to start the building.

We didn't have a thing to live in. This one friend, he let us have a sheep wagon, a little bed in one end and one of them little tiny stoves. Then along come winter! We didn't have this place built up enough so you could live in it without freezin' to death. I had to go and stay in Roy most of the time. My son was in school; I was workin' in the restaurant.

My husband was out here, and the winter was gettin' worse and worse. Gee, if you spilled a little water on the floor in that sheep wagon, it'd freeze before you could grab somethin' to wipe it up. Russell and his man who's tryin' to help stayed in it for quite a while, but the winter kept gettin' worse. They went over to the neighbors and stayed, but their house was small and they had some kids, so they'd take the mattress and sleep on the floor. They'd have to put it outdoors in the daytime because there wasn't room in the house. When they'd get it at night to lay on it, it was so cold they just shivered 'til pert near morning. And then it was time to get up again.

That winter of '49 and '50 was one of the worst winters we've had here. This country was all open, no fences from here to Roy. People's cattle drifted in here and died down by the corral. The men was tryin' to get some of them up, but it was a hopeless thing. They were starving and freezing.

A lot of people lost cattle, a whole lot of cattle. The river had an ice jam, ice blocked up, and some of the few head of cattle we had got out on the ice jam and were lost. We was right back to almost nuthin' again. From then on, it's been year after year, a few good ones, and a few very bad ones.

I was thinkin' the other day, all these years I've never lived in a house where they've had a bathroom. My folks had to get along that way. Every house we moved in wasn't equipped.

When we got here, no use in havin' a bathroom, we didn't have water. Now that I could, I don't know where I'd put it. I thought I'd fix that porch up and put it there. I had a man out here and asked him. He said, "What about the water line? Your water comes in over *here*." There was always something too complicated.

Someone said, "You can't saw through these logs. You'd weaken the house. The roof comes down and makes it hard to add on. I don't know how you'd manage that roof." And then I look at this house—it's settling crooked—and I think it's hardly worth it. I keep gettin' along without the bathroom. I need a new house!

I've got a bathtub out there [in a small metal building]. Last fall we put the lawn mower and stuff in there. I've got to get things straightened around so I can go out and take a bath. The water's kind of cold; you have to heat it up a bit. I was goin' to get a heater you drop in, like one of those you use to heat a tank for cattle. I was a little afraid that someone might do somethin' wrong, electrocute theirselves. Myself, I would just disconnect it.

I had it lookin' nice. You could sit on the couch, the bathtub was there, and a little stand to put your stuff on. It gets real hot out there, that metal building with skylights and the sun shinin' down.

I wanted to make a shower. I bought a metal trash can. I thought if I filled it up with water and got it up on a stand, I would have the shower right over the tub. The sun would warm the water. I don't know how to get it through the shed to make the shower, but I could get somebody to help me. I've got a lot of ideas, but they don't materialize.

When we first came here, there wasn't any water. They'd had a little dam over the hill. It would hold water in the spring when there'd be the most moisture. For drinkin' water that's all there was. We used to have to haul all our drinkin' water. I never wanted to drink out of them little potholes or dams.

We finally got a cistern built and caught rainwater. We put a little pitcher pump in the kitchen, and we pumped water out of that. We never liked to drink it, but sometimes we had to.

When we'd go to Lewistown, we always took a cream can along. We'd bring drinkin' water home. We'd go in to Roy and get some, but some of that water was so alkali you could hardly drink it. Some wells got polluted because of seepage—the well was so close to the street. Those wells weren't very deep, and it got so they weren't healthy. The railroad had a deeper well, and people used to get water there.

We've had a couple of years, all the dams went dry. It was hard on the stock. We got some of them dry this year; but we've got some wells drilled now. They just finished one down there on the corner of my place.

I give an easement so everybody's stock can go over there and get a drink. We'd been furnishin' everybody water for years. We's one of the first ones to get a well drilled down on Armells [Creek]. We never did fence people's stuff away from it. We fixed a little corral where you could brand some calves and have a water gap where everybody's stuff could go up and get a drink. It's a dandy little well, and it was one of the first in the area.

Another well is drilled by that building there, and we got a pipe that comes down to the house. Through the ASCS [Agricultural Stabilization and Conservation Service] . . . you got some kind of help on the cost. You had to put it where you're goin' to use it for your stock, or they wouldn't help you pay to drill the well.

It's artesian, you don't have to have a pump on it; it's warm, and it stays open all winter. It's a deep well, pretty close to eighteen hundred feet. Every time I take a drink of that water, I thank God we got this well. It's good water, you couldn't have anything better, couldn't have anything do you more good than that water.

The water has been the blessing to this country. People can say what they want, but if it wasn't for the water, you wouldn't have all you got now. The water's the main thing.

One summer it was terribly dry. My husband was away workin' for one of those [crews] puttin' in a big power highline out on the coast, my son was away, and I was here alone. The dams was all dry. I rode out there . . . quite a few bunches of horses frantically pawing in one of them little places along the coulee. I gathered up what I could and drove them clear down on Armells Creek where there was a little water in one of them dams, but not a lot. I got them down there, and then I come back and got another bunch. I gathered up two little bunches of cattle, made two trips from Fargo Coulee all the way down there to Slim's old shack that had metal up the side of it. They made a run for that; they thought it was water. They see that glistening. I got 'em over to one little dam, and it helped them for a few days.

It's terrible to see animals so thirsty they're frantic. I never seen horses like that before nor since. Their sides were drawed up; they were pawin' like mad, tryin' to get down to a little moisture to get a drink. I thought we'd have to sell everything. I called my son to come and help. Mr. Finkle [a neighbor] had a big dam, and he didn't have any cattle. He said, "If you want to fix the fence, you can put 'em in there."

We gathered like mad gettin' 'em in. One old cow, she was so weak. I don't know how many times we'd go on with some of the others and come back, and there she'd be, bogged down and too weak to move her to cover. We had to try to get her a drink until we could do something else with her.

We finally gathered all we could and got 'em over to Mr. Finkle's dam. After they'd been there a little while, it started to rain, and by leavin' 'em there a little bit, we got 'em back out to our own land.

At first I didn't like ranching. I thought, gee, I don't know if I want to tie myself to this. I guess it took me 'bout three years to understand why anybody would want to come here. It was so hot, and we had this little plot and this dumpy little old house. I couldn't see the future. I couldn't get it through my head how we's ever goin' to have anything or what the future was.

But after while your roots got to growin' and you got started . . . thought you'd make a go of this thing. You tried to get a little more land. From then on, you got to gettin' a little more, seemed you might make somethin'. We got so far in debt one time, tryin' to get a little more land, tryin' to build these dams, the PCA [Production Credit Association] wouldn't lend us any more money. We went over to the bank and told them our situation. They come out and looked to see whatcha had, how many cattle you could run, how much money you wanted.

They staked us, and we kept creepin' ahead, creepin' a little bit ahead until we got paid out, so we didn't have interest to pay. Kept on goin', a little more and a little more until we got up to where we are now.

You gotta make yourself like it, make up your mind you was goin' to stick to it. There was no halfway deal. If you couldn't make up your mind to sell out, you'd better stay with it.

We had one old milk cow, but there was the job of findin' her every day and gettin' her up here. It wasn't hardly worth it.

I used to ride out in the evening and bring her up to the shed to milk her. Sold a little milk to a neighbor. I charged her a nickel a quart. Didn't get rich a-doin' that. She gave me a thing to put the milk in, a little bit short of a quart. I filled it as full as I could. Then she got to givin' me a little bit bigger dish. I filled that just about as full. And then she gave me *another* dish, a little bigger. It was kind of amusing.

I used to bring her mail up. She couldn't get around to walk very good. Then she wanted me to paint her kitchen. I wasn't really hankerin' for this job. I used to paint my own, but I was never a painter for anybody else.

Well, I give it a try. I got up there and was paintin' away, tryin' to do the best I could, and she'd set there, "Well, there's a little spot over there. Could be a little more over here."

I finally got it done. She paid a little, very little. She was a good old soul, but kind of tight on the money. I never said anything. I was tight myself. It wasn't enough to cry about. What's a quart of milk? At the time, I thought, oh, gosh, do I have to do this? But now it's kind of laughable.

In the early years, lots of times we'd come home—you never locked the doors—and find the beds all full. Somebody'd come ridin' in, fixed themselves somethin' to eat, and went to bed. I've come home and found a whole row of boots settin' outside the door. It was nothin' uncommon to come home and find your house full of somebody.

Bea credited the wells and the dams they built with an increase in the wildlife population in the area. Sometimes she enjoyed seeing the animals, and other times they were a nuisance.

We see more wildlife than we did in them years when there was no water here. Water is what's made the wild game 'n' that come. But those dry years, before they got the dams built, you had to go hunt to find a deer.

Down on the river they had those little whitetails, but they're smaller, not like these mule deers. Some antelope hang down the road. There's quite a few antelope down in there. They're friendly until towards huntin' season, and they begin to get more scary. They sure seem to know. And they know people, too. They know whether you're going to hurt them. A lot of them got used to our old rattly black pickup that made a lot of noise. They wouldn't run, and the thing was makin' enough noise to scare 'em out of the country.

I've never shot at a deer in all the years I've lived here. Sometimes I've been so mad at 'em I could whack 'em over the head with a club. I set some little trees out, and they'd come up in the yard at night and eat all the leaves off. Then they'd hop over the fence into a little place where I've had tomatoes and strawberries. They'd eat what they wanted; I could take what's left.

I wake up in the morning, and a whole bunch of deer layin' right in front of the door. I run out there with a sheet one day, a-wavin' it. I was gonna scare 'em. I nearly scared the horses out of the horse lot. They went up with their heads, about to take off. The deer just run over the fence, turned around, and looked atcha. Didn't even run out of sight. Got out of the yard a little bit and stood there. But the horses nearly went frantic from me rushin' out, wavin' that sheet, the wind a-blowin'.

The other day I was in that yellow pickup and a blame little bluebird was bound he was goin' to come right in there with me. I had the window down, I reached out my hand, and he fluttered around. He almost lit on my hand. He set there and looked at himself in the lookin' glass [outside rearview mirror]. He didn't go until I started the pickup and went to drive off. I never heard of a little bluebird gettin' so tame.

I like birds, but sometimes I get kinda mad at them robins. They yelp around, and if you've got a strawberry or something somewhere, they're in there eatin' it. They're hard on stuff that way. You can't keep 'em out.

But the little bluebirds don't seem to hurt anything. I like them and the little yellow canaries [goldfinches]. They're such happy little things. They've got a sweet song, really nice. I always try to scare the cats away if I think they're goin' to catch one. We used to put tin around a tree, build a birdhouse, and set it above the tin so the cat can't climb the tree. But lately I've got too many things to do. I can't seem to get everything done.

Living alone in Bea's isolated situation would tax the strength and ingenuity of the best of us. Winters can be especially trying.

I've been snowed in when I've been here alone. Walked from here to the neighbors [a distance of more than two miles] with some mail I needed to get out. Then I tried to walk back and got into a snowdrift. I thought I wasn't gonna make it back here. It got dark, and it was one blanket of snow. Not even a rabbit track. You couldn't tell where the road was; you kinda knew the general direction. I didn't know enough to keep out of them deep drifts. I got in one drift that was waist deep, and I thought, this is it. I'm gettin' tired, and it's too deep to get my foot up to step over. I don't know whether I'm goin' to rest a while or what.

I kept on goin' and come to find out I was a little closer to the house than I thought I was. I moved out of that deep drift and got up here.

Another trip, I went with the horse. The horse got flounderin' in the snow. I thought, well, this is *really* it. She's gonna fall down, fall right on me. I finally got there. The neighbor's nephew—I had never met him—was there alone. He had me come in, took my horse and tied it up, and fixed me some tea. They'd brought my mail that far, and I left mail to go. I had tea with him, then he goes out and gets my horse ready and helped me, and I'd never seen the young fellow before! He was really nice. I got home, but I don't know which was worse, tryin' to walk, or take the horse.

There's been years when the snow would get deep, and it'd get an inch of hard crust. The cows' legs had the hair all wore off on the back from punchin' down through that crusted snow. It's hard on 'em; they can't get their noses down to eat, can't break through that crust. A few of them was down there where the horses was. The horses would paw, and they would find a little grass, but not much.

We had some really mean things happen. You get to thinkin' about all the bad, sometimes I wonder if you ever think about the good.

I don't hardly go to town if the weather's bad. I try to get in to do somethin' about Christmas. I didn't get all my stuff done last year. In bad years, if I got there twice through the whole winter, I'd be doin' good. I usually have enough food. Might not be everything you want, but you never get caught without something.

In the summer I go, well, really, just when I have to.
I never seem to go on pleasure trips. I haven't even got
straightened up with my accountant over my income
tax. He hasn't sent me the bill, and I haven't got my
papers yet. I don't know how much I made last year.

It's been funerals the last two times I've been in
town. And then I do what business I can on the side. It
seems like the only time I get anywhere is if somebody's
sick or a funeral or I simply have to go for somethin'. No
pleasure trips.

I've never been on a vacation in my life. The only
time I've ever went anywhere . . . going back to my
mother's funeral [in Minnesota]. No, I never had a
vacation in my whole life.

At eighty, Bea was still branding her own calves with a brand
she had created herself.

I call my brand a Spear B, a spear and a B for my first
name. That's the way I read it. I figured it out myself
and wrote in to the Department of Brands.

I did some branding this spring. Whenever I happened to go out and get a few calves in, I branded them
up alone. I woulda done more, but I was busy and I
didn't get around to getting any more in. When they get
too big, it's not only ropin' 'em and gettin' 'em tied down,
it's a-lettin' 'em loose. Sometimes they take right to ya.

A year ago I had some help. Friends of Rocky [Bea's
grandson], all settin' around on the fence, women and
children, all visitin' and havin' a good time. I was in there

gettin' the branding done, and this one was on the fight. He's a pretty good size, halfway between a calf and a yearling. Wilder than heck, runnin' around, ready to take anything that moved. I was goin' to head for the fence to crawl up so he wouldn't hit me. He was a-snortin' and a-comin'. I turned my back, and he sent me headlong into the fence. I didn't have time to get scared. My face was bleedin' from wood slivers. It cut my lip, cut through here, and the blood was a-runnin' down. There's a little scar there yet. My legs got weak; I felt like I wanted to tip over. Rocky, my grandson, came in and carried me out of the corral. I got back on my feet and went to work again. I never quit workin'; I never went to a doctor.

I try to judge if it was me gettin' branded. You know it hurts. You try not to hurt 'em any more than you have to. I don't hold the iron there any longer than I can help, just enough so it's goin' to stay on and show.

I've seen some of them give 'em a kick when they get up. And laugh. I don't like to see animals abused. Once in a while you have to haul off and whack one, but I don't like it. You can handle them a lot easier if you're nice to them. I can go out there and walk a bunch of 'em in the corral. If somebody comes out, one of these that handles 'em fast and takes a run at 'em, they'll scatter and go ever' direction. Once in a while, you'll get one like people, hard to manage. . . .

One time we was gatherin' horses, tryin' to get 'em up to the house to corral 'em. My husband was drivin' 'em, and I was tryin' to head 'em this way. We had a little stallion in the bunch, and they're always a little behind.

I was tryin' to get ahead of the mares. My horse, he fell goin' downhill, and his rear end come right up in the air. I fell halfway on my back. I tried to shove myself away from him, but he come down on my knee and crushed my leg. When I went to turn over, the foot was headed one way, and I was headed the other.

It broke it right in two, and the bones come out through the side of my leg. The stud horse, he went off a little way and stood there and nickered. My horse, when he finally got to his feet, he stood there, too. Never tried to leave.

My husband come up to the house and got a short piece of iron and one of my best pillows, a big down pillow my grandmother had given me. He wrapped it around my leg, blood running out. He fixed me so he could get me in the pickup. I don't remember how he managed; I suppose I hopped on one leg. When we got to Lewistown, that pillow was soaked with blood. I wonder I didn't bleed to death.

The doctor took the pillow off. I could feel the blood runnin' all the way down my leg. I kept tellin' him, "Don't pull my foot off." I was afraid when he took my boot off he was goin' to pull my foot off. I didn't want to lose my leg. "Cut it," I said. "Cut it up the side." He ripped the seam up the side and took it off. He took the boot upside down and poured blood out. The pillow was soaked through and through. I got a scar there yet where the bone come out. I was in the hospital for over six weeks.

The next year after that bad break, I was helpin' my husband. It was muddy. I slipped and broke my leg below the knee. The same leg, it cracked like you break a stick. Didn't splinter like that other one.

We went in that day, and the doctor said it wasn't broke. There were so many lines from the other break he thought it wasn't broke, just hurt.

"Go home and stay off of it."

I come home, and for eleven days I couldn't even get in bed without takin' hold of it, liftin' the leg up. I was hobblin' around. I thought, it ain't gettin' any better. I can't go on like this. I went back, and I told him, "I'm sure it must be broke." He looked again. "Well, yeah," he said. "It is." He put a cast across there so it'd hold it in place. It got better after that. But for a long time I couldn't get to bed without gettin' a-hold of my foot and liftin' it up.

I always wonder how much doctors really know. Like once when I went. "Oh," he said, "there's a lot of old people have that trouble." And I was supposed to go back again. I thought, Well, to heck! If old people have this trouble, why should I go back? I took care of it myself.

Looking back over the years, I don't know how many times we've given this place a start. You think you've got it made, and then you're back to the bottom. You've got to climb right back up again. Luck's been with me the last few years. We haven't had them bad winters. I could have lost the whole works, bein' here alone.

Last year I was out there pullin' some of them ninety-pound bales and tryin' to load 'em [into the pickup]. When they get wet, they're harder than ever to move around. I tore the muscles loose in this arm. I've got a lump; the muscle kinda knotted and tore loose. I did ask the doctor if he could fix it. He said, "Well, if it don't bother you, you could just leave it." It don't really bother, only I don't feel as strong in that arm. Ever' once in a while, when I lift something, it'll hurt a little bit. I'm gettin' 'bout to the limit. I'm gettin' too many years on me to keep a-goin'.

You don't get no Saturday or Sunday, no holiday, no vacation. It's every day and every day. If I'm not goin' to keep enough [cattle] to make it pay, make it pay good, what's the use?

I used to be kinda afraid when you had to light them old kerosene lamps. I always hated comin' in the house. I had an eerie feelin', wonderin' if somebody was in there. But now that you can snap on the light, it don't bother me. I always had a kind of wonderin'... look under the bed, look in the corners. It don't bother me anymore.

There're a lot of things I don't know, and I should take more time and take a few hours off and read. But don't you think the country's gettin' more like a Sodom and Gomorrah outfit? It's just a good time: sports and relaxation, everything for pleasure. There really isn't any serious thought about the hereafter, or what's keepin' this whole country a-goin'. Or have time to look around and be thankful, for whatever you have, like that water, the trees. I think people just figure they owe it to 'em. You got it, you should have it, never think with the snap of your finger everything could be gone. You never appreciate the things—I don't say all people, a lot of them do, but there's a lot of them never give it a thought. Just a good time, that's about all they're lookin' at.

There for a while, my husband and I used to drive into Lewistown to go to church, until they got to changin' ministers so much. For a while they didn't have one, and then we kinda got away. I think you got to be one of the bunch; just goin' very seldom, it don't work out. If you're not one of the bunch or can't keep up with 'em, you kind of lose interest, but I always did believe in the hereafter. I believe there's a little more than just yourself.

One thing I never got to doin', talkin' to myself. Sometimes I'll be standin' there lookin' out the window and drift off into thoughts, thinkin' different things. It's like goin' to a movie, only it goes through your mind, thinkin' and seein' things, livin' 'em over in your mind. I spend a lot of time like that. I guess that's why I don't get so lonesome. I can drift off into the past thinkin' about things. The time goes by. . . .

Bea Murray was interviewed at her home in Roy, Montana, in May 1988. She died there in January 2003. She was ninety-seven years old.

ABOUT THE AUTHORS

A native of Illinois, DONNA GRAY began her work in oral history while living in the Bay Area of California. With her husband's retirement in the mid-1970s, the couple bought a ranch in Montana's Paradise Valley, where Donna became interested in the histories of neighboring ranch wives. That interest prompted her to expand her search for the stories of Montana's rural women.

LINDA PEAVY and URSULA SMITH, who contributed the foreword, have been working in women's history for thirty years. They have coauthored ten books, including *Pioneer Women* and *Women in Waiting in the Westward Movement*.